MW00461251

Praise for *The Language of the Soul*

Open-hearted, accessible, and drawn from deep wells of reflection, this lovely book about the longings we know but can sometimes barely name offers solace and hope. We are not alone in our longings; they are what we share most deeply. And the beginning of fulfillment lies in the longing itself. Jeff Crosby's years of wide reading and rich conversation with Christian writers are reflected in the moments of encounter and voices he invokes in story after story about longings that have brought both the ache of the "not yet" and the assurance of things not seen that enables us to rejoice in the midst of our waiting and wondering. This book is worth reading slowly, as an invitation to feel and reflect on our own deepest longings and where they may lead us.

Marilyn McEntyre, author of *Where the Eye Alights* and *Word by Word*

This is one of the finest books I have ever read. Crosby's humility and insight, along with his vast expertise and diverse interests, point the way toward authentic transformation and hope. Here you will find embodied, practical wisdom located in place, music, story, literature, friendship, nature, faith, and spirituality.

Mark R. McMinn, coauthor of *A Time for Wisdom*

What appears to be untranslatable in our interior lives is broadly and wisely interpreted here in this important book: We long to be loved. If God is love, we long for God. Read with gratitude as Jeff Crosby guides us to fully understand our spiritual, physical, and emotional longings.

Christopher de Vinck, author of *The Power of the Powerless: A Brother's Legacy of Love* and *Simple Wonders*

Sometimes our longings and discontent make us feel like we are not growing spiritually—*when will we ever be satisfied?*—but Jeff Crosby's work in *The Language of the Soul: Meeting God in the Longings of Our Hearts* reframes longing as a *way* to grow. With transparency and wisdom, Crosby walks us through the longings that show we are human and reminds us of the God who meets us right in those very spots, and often through the beauty of community. Pay attention to your *saudade*. Then read this lovely book.

Karen Stiller, author of *The Minister's Wife: A Memoir of Faith, Doubt, Friendship, Loneliness, Forgiveness, and More,* senior editor, *Faith Today* magazine, Ontario, Canada

Through multiple references the author implicitly opens up channels for the reader to see, name, and ponder how the ten longings he describes shape the reader's own life. This is a book to cherish, re-read, and discuss in small groups, It is especially suited for those who are humbly honest about their own longings, and who want to understand, and perhaps even refine them.

Gregory Clapper, author of *When the World Breaks Your Heart*

Writing a book that seeks to define an undefinable word takes someone who is willing to rely on God's wisdom and not their own, who can trust the small voice that speaks to them as they write and above all who is kind to their readers and themselves in the process. Jeff Crosby is such a person. In *The Language of the Soul* he introduces us to a new word that describes an ancient and ever new experience: the longing, burning heart.

Michael Card, singer/songwriter and author of *A Sacred Sorrow*

Throughout my life, I have felt, but been unable to name, the longings Jeff Crosby identifies in this marvelous book. Now I have a name for this universal condition: *saudade*. It is a gift to know this word and to discover myself in these pages. You'll discover yourself too. Jeff Crosby weaves together the deep longings of our hearts and souls and leads us to places of healing, wholeness, and rest. *The Language of the Soul* is a wonderful piece of spiritual writing.

Jeff Munroe, author of *Reading Buechner*

Longing is more than emotion. It is a spiritual landscape that is both familiar and largely unexplored. Jeff Crosby has written an engaging field guide that describes its contours and helps us navigate ten core longings that we experience on the spiritual journey. You won't find a better guide than Crosby, who speaks from broad experience with appealing honesty. Spend some time with him and see how longing for the home you've never had, sitting on a lawn tractor, or the daily grind of your job can all be contexts where God instills in you a desire for him. You will find that, instead of being a place of unfulfilled desire and disappointment, the landscape of longing is the landscape of hope.

John Koessler, author of *The Radical
Pursuit of Rest* and *Practicing the Present*

Jeff Crosby is a faithful Christ-follower, a transparent apprentice, a kind-hearted CEO, an attentive husband, father, and grandfather, and my beloved friend. All of this will be self-evident to those who read this book. *The Language of the Soul* will be a helpful tool in guiding you through your own longings of the heart. This is necessary reading.

J. K. Jones, author of *A Missing Discipleship:
What the Monks and Nuns Can Teach Us*

What comes through in this book is the reality that Jeff Crosby is pointing the way toward becoming a full and whole person. Not simply a writer or a leader, but a person who has learned well how to live a life integrated with God. To read this book is to be invited to engage with your own longings, hopes, and dreams along with the compassionate Spirit. Jeff gives us a gift through good, honest writing and a tremendous sense of what it means to live fully and wholly here and now.

Casey Tygrett, spiritual director and
author of *The Gift of Restlessness*

In a world always striving for more, I tend to see my longings through a consumer lens of discontent. *The Language of the Soul* gave me a word to describe longings that come from a very different place: the ones not compromised by selfishness or ego. The richness of these ten longings provides me new ways to imagine the part I get to play in the kingdom.

Jon Hirst, cofounder of Generous Mind
and coauthor of *Innovation in Mission*

Jeff Crosby's reflections on "the longings of our heart" are both inspiring and practical. Inspiring, in that his evocative storytelling invites readers to find their own experience in his. Practical, in that he provides a framework for considering how our vast longings—for home and community and balance—can lead us toward a deeper faith. Crosby shows how these *longings* are a central part of our *being*, and that only by accepting and understanding them, can we find the spiritual *belonging* that we seek.

Tom Montgomery Fate, author of *Cabin Fever*

THE LANGUAGE
OF THE SOUL

THE LANGUAGE
OF THE SOUL

MEETING GOD IN THE
LONGINGS OF OUR HEARTS

Jeff Crosby

Broadleaf Books
Minneapolis

For Cindy
"All my life. Without a doubt, I give you all my life."

CONTENTS

Foreword by Suzanne Stabile   xi

Introduction: *Saudade*—Listening to the Longings
    of Our Hearts   xvii

Part I: Our Interior Longings

Chapter 1: The Longing for Home   3

Chapter 2: The Longing for an Undivided Life   17

Chapter 3: The Longing for Freedom from Fear
    and Anxiety   33

Chapter 4: The Longing for Forgiveness   51

Chapter 5: The Longing for Spiritual Transformation   69

Chapter 6: The Longing for Peace   85

Part II: Our Exterior Longings

Chapter 7: The Longing for Community   103

Chapter 8: The Longing for Friendship   117

Chapter 9: The Longing for Meaningful Work   131

Part III: Our Eternal Longings

Chapter 10: The Longing for Heaven   151

Epilogue   165

Afterword by James Bryan Smith   173

Questions for Personal Reflection and Group Discussion   179

Gratitudes   185

Notes   189

Recommended Reading for Further Study and Reflection   199

Saudade — A vague and constant desire for something that does not and possibly cannot exist, for something other than the present, a turning toward the past or toward the future; not an active discontent or poignant sadness but an indolent dreaming wistfulness.

FOREWORD

Suzanne Stabile

I first met Jeff Crosby in 2015, then the publisher at Inter-Varsity Press, on the occasion of signing a contract with the press for the publication of my first book, *The Road Back to You*, coauthored with Ian Morgan Cron. I found him to be a consummate professional, but there was more.

As we all talked of writing and books and publishing, Jeff made room for every voice, leading us through dinner with palpable humility and grace. Jeff wore kindness like an old but favorite sweater. You know, the style with leather buttons and patches on the sleeves so they would both stand the test of time. It was a kindness that only accompanies those who have chosen to be vulnerable enough to allow life to change them in some significant way. On the way back to our hotel, my husband Joe and I commented that it would be a privilege to one day count Jeff among our friends. And it has proven to be an even greater blessing than we imagined.

I suppose every person's relationship with words is necessarily unique. While I'm honored to have three books published,

I'm a teacher who happens to write books, which is very different from a writer who teaches. I have a deep need to put words together so that when they are spoken they will convey exactly the idea that I have in mind. Meaningful conversation is my only path to the places in my heart and soul that are hard to reach. But music and lyrics are the way to Jeff's soul. And thank God for that because if it were not so, we might have missed the gift of being introduced to this book and to an understanding of *saudade*.

Jeff writes, "The mesmerizing word came to me first, as so many things have, through music. Though I have worked in the world of books since 1983, music is the language of my soul."

He continues, "But *this* word. It was an unfamiliar, beguiling term, and the music it was connected to sounded passionate and evoked at once a sense of wonder, reflection, mystery, and allure." His fascination with the meaning of *saudade* is the basis for the irresistible stories that are the heart of this beautiful book. With a gentle voice and abundant grace Jeff names those parts of our lives that are necessarily defined by our understanding of longing. And then with oh so much courage he leads us to our own empty spaces that long to be healed by sharing his.

It has been my experience that good teachers and accomplished writers of nonfiction have at least this one thing in common. They describe for us things that we know to be true but are unable to name for ourselves. Perhaps the reason I have come to love this book so much is because Jeff has given me language for feelings that I carry with me everywhere I go but have struggled to name. And I promise it will do the same for you.

This intriguing and beautiful word represents more depth than breadth. It is more expansive than reductive. And for those who are curious, it initiates conversations about longing and loving, and forgiveness and grace. *Saudade* is very personal. It's a word that knows the places in our hearts that are not really broken and yet in need of healing. And perhaps the greatest gift of all is that it is immensely helpful for those of us who want to share with those we love, the stories that are our lives.

Saudade

Whenever we listen to the loamy contralto
of Virginia Rodrigues, singing of blackness and exile

and the warm seas of Bahia, the neighbor's dog and I
stare at the speakers, full of sadness and desire.

Bruno is an Italian greyhound; we are mostly white;
we live in city apartments and do not speak
    Portuguese.

Still, something in the singer's ineluctable rhythms,
her long vowels like a beautiful howling, seems
    familiar,

and I know the way Bruno feels when I turn to
    address him,
his eyes fixed in anxious concentration, as though
    English

were a language he has inexplicably forgotten,
but will recover, as soon as he remembers how to fold

his long tongue into a ship that will ferry him out
of the taut wedge of a body in which he has been
   detained,

back to his native land. There, from the corporeal lap
of the sofa, whose back is the green coast of Salvadór,

whose arms, the beautiful, burdened arms of Africa,
he will reply, "Is the samba not proof that all possible

worlds are united in this one?" *Oh sim, certamente,*
I'll say, the music swelling around us like the slow

respiring sea, that is here and there, then and now,
and has been singing forever.

Jennifer Maier
from *Now, Now*

Introduction

Saudade—Listening to the Longings of Our Hearts

The music of your life is subtle and elusive and like no other—not a song with words but a song without words, a singing, clattering music to gladden the heart or turn the heart to stone, to haunt you perhaps with echoes of a vaster, farther music of which it is part.

Frederick Buechner, "The Sacred Journey"

The mesmerizing word came to me first, as so many things have, through music. Though I have worked in the world of books since 1983, music is the language of my soul. I suspect it will always be so.

But *this* word. It was an unfamiliar, beguiling term, and the music it was connected to sounded passionate and evoked at once a sense of wonder, reflection, mystery, and allure.

Saudade. Over the course of some forty years of listening, the word appeared repeatedly in samba, jazz, fado, and bossa nova music associated with artists such as Jáo Gilberto, Ivan Lins, Stan Getz, the Jack DeJohnette Trio, Antônio Carlos Jobim, Oscar Castro-Neves, Chick Corea, Gary Burton, Yo-Yo Ma, Adriano Correia de Oliveira, and many others—much of it emanating from Brazil or musicians influenced by its culture. Later, pop, rock, and blues artists like Southern California's Stephen Bishop, Britain's Chris Rea, Australia's Nick Cave, and Holland's Jan Akkerman recorded songs using the same word or exploring its themes, but without explanation. In the digital age, the word has its own Spotify channel, multiple playlists, and hundreds of returns on a keyword search.

Saudade. What did it mean? What was the root of its allure? It seemed to be a word with some special significance.

As one who has worked with words for a living all my adult life, understanding the roots and meaning of *saudade* became something of a challenge, a fascination. In the pre-Google era of my early quest, it wasn't easy to find information. But over time a story or a *feeling*, a sense, began to come into view. As I learned more, the interest in *saudade* deepened and I began to make connections to my own spiritual journey.

A Portuguese word, it's pronounced *sow-dodge-ee* and is among the words that linguists label "untranslatable." Most descriptions speak of it as a vague and constant desire for something, someplace, or someone that does not and perhaps cannot exist; a yearning for something other than the present; a turning toward the past or toward the future. Writers have suggested it does not describe an active discontent or poignant sadness as much as an indolent, dreaming wistfulness.

The word reflects "a melancholic longing or nostalgia for a person, place or thing that is far away either spatially or in time," says David Robson, "a vague, dreaming wistfulness for phenomena that may not even exist."

Definitions like these can sound distant and unapproachable. But when I uttered the word to my friend Joaquim, who hails from the city of Assis Chateaubriand in Brazil, asking about *his* understanding of *saudade*, tears filled his eyes. The connection was immediate and deep and anything but distant.

"I'm so glad you know that word. It's a beautiful, rich word," Joaquim told me. "It's not mere nostalgia. Brazilians use it in a way that is far beyond just remembering the past. It's a part of their present. It's a word that is spoken at least once a day by an average Portuguese-speaking person. It's a picture of how their past informs and is intertwined with their present."

To make a connection familiar to both of us, Joaquim mentioned the biblical story from Luke 24. The story follows the account of Christ's resurrection, as two men are walking on the road to Emmaus. To Joaquim, it is a walk connected to a sense of *saudade*. As they walk the resurrected Jesus meets them on the road. Yet neither recognized him. It is only after Jesus takes leave of them that the two men said, "Were not our hearts burning within us while he was talking to us on the road, while he was opening the scriptures to us?" (Luke 24:32).

"When we talk about the feeling of *saudade*," Joaquim continued, "to me it feels like therapy, a reset, a deep thoughtful moment. When their hearts were burning within them, they were feeling *saudade* for Jesus." As he spoke his voice rippled with animation, his eyes filled with moisture. "Maybe that's why the two men strongly urged Jesus to linger with them, saying, 'Stay with us!' And when their eyes were opened and in an instant they saw Jesus, their *saudade* was 'killed' just a bit, as we say in my country, because suddenly Jesus vanished from their sight. But it gave them a burst of energy and they could not contain themselves, so they ran back to Jerusalem to share the good news."

Joaquim's words remind me how often I read the Bible through a distinctly North American lens, and how rich it is to read it through the eyes of other cultures. Brazilian culture, where the word *saudade* is a daily companion of the people, is one in which feelings are felt deeply and exhibited in an unrestrained manner. As Joaquim put it, Brazilian people dig down and allow themselves to be in touch with what is there, to ponder it, to experience it.

Perhaps the distinctions between Joaquim's culture and mine, which is marked more by stoicism than an easy expression of emotions, gives us a clue why there is no English translation for *saudade*, as is commonly understood.

A few years ago at a three-day spiritual retreat with the author Parker J. Palmer and musician Carrie Newcomer, I met a woman who has for more than twenty-five years been a lay missionary in several locations far from her native Queens, New York, including South Africa, Brazil, and now Argentina.

Most retreatants there had traveled just a few hours by car to the gathering, but she had traveled days and through multiple airports to get there. For that determination and for her striking attentiveness to others, she stood out to all of us gathered in that retreat center in Wisconsin.

When we spoke, Heidi Maria Schmidt recalled her time in Brazil, attending a three-month language school where she and two dozen other people learned Portuguese.

"I remember a curious word that appeared early on in our classes—*saudade*. Any Brazilian who tried to explain it assured us that it was a particular word for Brazilians that didn't have a proper translation in any other language," Schmidt told me. "It alludes to missing, longing, but is much more complex. I was intrigued."

Having lived continents away from family, friends, language, familiar food, song, dance, and culture for such a long time, Schmidt says that during her time in Brazil she could glimpse at least a small measure of such yearning for something deep, for things that formed her into who she is today, "where a smell, a song on the radio, hearing the sounds of a familiar accent, finding a familiar brand in the store could trigger a sudden surge of intense longing that crept up from the deepest of places."

It was in Brazil that Schmidt began her slow but persistent understanding of such an experience as *saudade*. "It is always there, deep down. And it can surface without warning. An unexpected trigger of a thousand things."

All of us carry, I'm convinced, deep-seated longings or yearnings in our hearts. It is how we are wired as people, whether we are conscious of it or not. And I've come to believe that being attentive to those longings, to understand what they are saying to us, is one of the markers of the with-God life.

Christian spirituality at its foundation, says Ronald Rolheiser in his book *The Holy Longing*, is about what we do with desire. "What we do with our longings, both in terms of handling the pain and the hope they bring us, that is our spirituality."

Within the longings of our hearts we do, indeed, meet both pain and hope in so many ways. Our longings are unique to each of us made in the *imago Dei*, the image of God. Some are, perhaps, universal and some are less common. But I have experienced ten such longings in a persistent, deep way:

- The longing for home
- The longing for an undivided self
- The longing for forgiveness received and extended
- The longing for friendship
- The longing for spiritual transformation
- The longing for peace
- The longing for community
- The longing to be freed from unhealthy fear and anxiety
- The longing for meaningful work
- The longing for heaven, our hearts' true home

In his perceptive wisdom, St. Augustine (354–430 CE), the North African theologian and philosopher, wrote that "longing is always at prayer even though the tongue is silent."

Such is my experience.

Memoirist, theologian, and novelist Frederick Buechner has been among the contemporary writers helping readers to listen to their lives—to be mindful of the longings of which Augustine wrote long before him, longings that are resident in the core of our being. In *Whistling in the Dark*, Buechner suggested, "Whenever you find tears in your eyes, especially unexpected tears, it is well to pay the closest attention. They are not only telling you something about the secret of who you are, but more often than not God is speaking to you through them of the mystery of where you have come from and is summoning you to where, if your soul is to be saved, you should go next."

In the pages that follow we will explore ten themes, many of which have brought unexpected tears to my eyes on a variety of occasions and have prompted me to notice, to pay attention to what they are saying. The longing for heaven—something decidedly in the future, however we regard its shape—stands distinct from the other nine, which are, you might say, my *saudades*: the wistful longings of what should be rather than what is; of what once was informing what I've carried with me to the present day; of what I hope—beyond words—to be true, one day.

And as I have paid attention, I have seen the ways in which God meets me, meets us all in ways unique to us, in our experience of our hearts' longings. As we journey together, we will be fellow travelers on a camino—on a path—called *saudade*. We do not travel the camino alone.

God is with us. And this is a shared human path.

My hope is that in these pages you will be connected to your own longings, and consider the ways in which you, too, have been—or, perhaps, may yet yearn to be—met through them by a God who knows you and calls you "beloved."

In the words of Psalm 38 we hear David's impassioned cry: "O Lord, all my longing is known to you; my sighing is not hidden from you." David's words arise out of his recognition of his own sin and its resulting distress. But his longing and sighing were known to God, and God remained with him.

Recognizing that reality—our brokenness and distress—let's journey on into ten longings of the heart. None of our sighs or longings are hidden from the one who created us and walks with us. *Thanks be to God.*

Saudade—Listening to the Longings of Our Hearts
A Playlist

"Saudade (Longing)," Oscar Castro-Neves with the Paul Winter Consort, from the recording *Oscar* (1987)

"Chega de Saudade," João Gilberto, from the recording *World Class Classics: João Gilberto* (2010)

"Saudades de Casa," Ivan Lins, from the recording *Saudades de Casa* (2007)

"Saudade," Nick Wolf, from the recording *Sunday Night Coffee* (2022)

"Saudade Part I and II," Chris Rea, from the recording *Chris Rea: The Very Best Of* (2001)

"Saudade," Gabriella Vargas Luna, from the recording *Saudade* (2021)

PART I

OUR INTERIOR LONGINGS

Ultimately, our yearning for God is the most
important aspect of our humanity, our most precious
treasure; it gives our existence meaning and direction.
Gerald G. May

CHAPTER 1

The Longing for Home

I was meant to walk these rails from the very first
day.
It gives me a sense of leaving without ever going
away.

Brooks Williams, "Railwalker"

The Indianapolis, Cincinnati, & Lafayette Railroad first came through the town of London, Indiana, in the late 1800s, carrying passengers, freight, livestock, and mail to and from the major cities of central Indiana and southwestern Ohio.

From that time and continuing through the 1930s London was home to a school, a seminary, and a grocery store with a US post office on the first floor and a dance hall directly above. The Cozy Nook Inn was on the edge of town (an interstate highway would displace the Inn in the 1950s) offering reasonably fine dining and clean rooms for its time and location, according to local lore. The town had a touring semi-pro basketball team and fielded an organized baseball squad named (of all things) the London Brooms. There were two train depots, a grain elevator, an interurban rail line connecting with other towns of the area, and a small white clapboard Methodist church.

Most of that was gone by the time I moved there in 1971 at the age of ten. The only commerce that remained was a small market where Ethel Bunce dispensed gasoline from two aging, rusted round-top fuel pumps outside and cold bottles of Coca-Cola, Mason's Root Beer, and Mountain Dew inside. On summer days and during the baseball season, she sold ice cream bars and Topps trading cards to the children of the community who congregated under the awning that covered the store's front porch. Nearby, the church was still standing, though I don't recall ever stepping inside. If on occasion the doors were open as I passed by, I would simply peer in out of curiosity, wondering, *What do they do in there on those uncomfortable-looking wooden benches?*

The railroad tracks were still there, used at least twice each day by what had by then become known as the Penn Central Railroad. The tracks were about forty yards away from the front porch of my home. I heard the train's whistle blow as it approached the London Road crossing, and I fantasized about hopping on board, like I'd seen scraggly-bearded men do in movies, and traveling to who knows where—anywhere but where I was, even if just for a few hours.

Many a day throughout all four Indiana seasons I walked those rails past the London Market and west a quarter of a mile to a decades-old wooden trestle that spanned Sugar Creek. I would climb into the underside of the bridge and walk across to a concrete pylon in the center of the creek. There, I would sit for what in my memory seems like hours, watching the water run far below and occasionally seeing the undercarriage of a freight train as it passed overhead, the rails moving up and down with the weight as the cars rolled by amid a thunderous cacophony of sound. With pen and paper I would scratch out my thoughts, a foreshadowing of a discipline that would begin in earnest later in life—journaling in order to be in touch with what I feel, and what I think.

That spot became my home away from home then, just a short jaunt down the tracks.

And in ways that are mysterious and paradoxical, the town and that railroad trestle, which still stands, are in some measure "home" to me still, deep in my bones even though I now live five hours away. In those days, I would walk the rails to give me a "sense of leaving without ever going away," in the words of the folk musician Brooks Williams. I couldn't wait to grow older, to leave, to find out what lay beyond the confines of that small town. And yet something about the place beckons to me more than fifty years later.

Home.

That paradox, I realize, is not unique to me. Perhaps you've experienced it as well?

"We are a people in the business of trying to recreate our homes," the writer and educator Christopher de Vinck says. "The greatest mission in our lives is to find our place. Where do we fit in? Where do we hang our coats in the evening?

From what window do we gaze out in the middle of the night and feel safe?"

Many years later, after moving away to college, marrying, and having two children and jobs that pulled me away to southern Indiana, Tennessee, and finally Illinois, I traveled back to London. Echoes of Simon and Garfunkel's song "My Little Town" and its refrain about "nothing but the dead and dying" being left there ran through my mind. It's an apt description of the town, and yet it holds a wellspring of memories that have never been shaken.

"To think about home eventually leads you to think back to your childhood home, the place where your life started," Frederick Buechner once said, "the place which off and on throughout your life you keep going back to if only in dreams and memories and which is apt to determine the kind of place inside yourself, that you spend the rest of your life searching for even if you are not aware that you are searching."

As I continue to search for home, continue to long to find home—in all its dimensions—in more profound and enduring ways, I am keenly aware God has met me along the way. Those longings for home, some would say, foreshadow a desire for heaven—the heart's true home. Maybe so, but I understand that longing for home is rooted deeply in our humanity. Our sense of home (or the lack of it) shapes who we are as people. Research scientist John S. Allen, in his exquisite study of the notion of home through the ages in *Home: How Habitat Made Us Human*, suggests the same. By his count, he lived in nineteen different dwellings in his lifetime, just one more than the count on my own list. And each of those physical dwellings, Allen writes, have been important touchstones for him with "a feeling of home [that] permeates my memories of [all of] them."

"Over the course of our lives," he says, "feeling at home provides cognitive continuity in the face of a surrounding environment that is highly variable and that we cannot control."

What do we make of this longing for home? At times I have felt my homesickness to be a curse, something to be avoided. At other times, I've received it as a gift propelling me to some new path, growth, exploration.

Many of us are restless wanderers trying to feel at home for the first time or recapture a sense of home that we have lost. M. Craig Barnes, a writer and seminary president, is familiar with this search. In his book *Searching for Home: Spirituality for Restless Souls*, he reflects on his own father's journey, which ended up with him very much alone, dying in a camping trailer. Barnes writes, "It doesn't matter how fervently the spiritualized among us protest that their souls have been saved, we all continue to wander through this life on the other side of the guarded gates of paradise, missing home."

If he's right, what do we do with what we are missing? As we navigate our lives and our longing for home, there are a number of avenues we can take.

Among the first truly deep male friendships I experienced was with Mark McMinn, a professor of psychology and author, as we met for years at a monthly breakfast, appropriately, at a railroad-themed diner. (Friendship is a separate longing I will consider in a subsequent chapter.) We'd meet at Danby's Station and talk about life, work, spirituality, family, and longing in a manner and depth I had rarely experienced. It was a challenge, then, when he informed me over scrambled eggs and toast one morning that he and his wife, Lisa, would be moving back to Oregon near where the two of them had grown up and first met.

McMinn's longing led to an uprooting and replanting in the soil (literally and figuratively) he and his family had come from, and they have flourished there.

"The drawback was the beauty of Oregon and the familiarity of the seasons, the geography, the friends, the culture," McMinn said. "We also longed to be part of the Friends (Quaker) church we had once been a part of."

McMinn and his wife found a small parcel of land where they grow the same fruit his grandfather harvested nearby two generations ago—strawberries, pears, apples, gooseberries. They live close to the soil, finding both physical and spiritual sustenance in the beauty and the seasons of the earth.

And yet, the longings persist.

"I recall Ronald Rolheiser's words, that life is an unfinished symphony. Even with all of the grace and beauty of this home, we have our unfulfilled longings that visit us from time to time," McMinn told me years after the move. "In a sense, we have learned to welcome these as our friends, too, knowing that these speak to the essence of being mortal and being human."

For him, returning to his native Oregon was a part of the answer to his longing for home.

Returning to the rural central Indiana of my childhood, however, didn't hold that true sense of home for me. An uprooting and replanting in the home of my youth will likely never happen, regardless of my nostalgic feelings for the place and the people I knew. Two of my six grandchildren live near my current residence. Community has been built in this place amid suburban sprawl over twenty-four years. I have taken paths at various crossroads that have led in different directions, and I regularly remind myself of the wise if often-overused challenge to "bloom where I'm planted." And so, the quenching of at least some aspects of this longing has taken other forms.

The notion of home in the Bible holds both a physical and a spiritual meaning, something that resonates for me as well. Years ago my wife and I began attending a liturgically oriented church for the first time, and I remember thinking (and feeling) as though I'd come home to a place I'd never set foot in before. It was as if I knew where all the furniture was located as I navigated the various rooms in the dark. The liturgy, with its structure of confession followed by the announcement of forgiveness alongside the Creeds, Lord's Prayer, Eucharist, and passing of the peace each week, became rooms in my spiritual home—places of belonging. It's one of the ways God has met me in this longing.

And there are others.

Home has become walks on a four-thousand-acre Nature Conservancy–owned tallgrass prairie with my naturalist wife, Cindy, watching (at considerable distance and on the other side of the fence!) American bison roam what had become a vanishing landscape of prairie and sustenance, now reintroduced and preserved.

Home has become quarterly gatherings of like-minded literary people in our home over a simple meal and conversation about books and the environment and how to make a difference in a world of strife and beauty, pain and opportunity.

Home has become winter walks through the spruce plot of a local arboretum, where the silence is amplified by the white bed below and the green canopy above.

Home has become solitary bike rides on the Illinois prairie path crafted out of an abandoned railroad bed.

Home is reading books to six grandchildren in person when we can, and through technology when we must.

Home. Even as our longings remain with us, we re-create home in this time of now-and-not-yet, and God meets us there as we are attentive to God's presence.

The ultimate expression of our longing for home is a yearning for heaven—a place we read about in Scripture, hear about in sermons, and perhaps read about in wildly imaginative books, some of dubious origin. Dubious origins or not, they relay a sense of true home, of arrival. Yet rarely have I taken the time to dwell on the subject at length. Recently, as I crossed the threshold of my sixtieth year, I've begun to think of it more often, and more deeply.

The Bible seems to speak of heaven in vague and multifaceted terms—part atmosphere surrounding the earth, part cosmic place, part "the dwelling place of God," as writer Douglas Connelly puts it in his book *The Promise of Heaven*.

The emotional truth of this ultimate longing for heaven as the yearning for home pressed into me a short time ago when

I walked through the doors of a Franciscan hospital less than thirty minutes from the London of my childhood.

For as long as I can recall my father was a restless soul, but that was especially true in his younger and mid-life years before his health limited his activity. His restlessness contributed significantly to the eighteen dwellings and moves I experienced—four in a single year. He was a man who fit M. Craig Barnes's declaration that "it doesn't matter where you move, how fast you run, or how many new identities you try on along the way, you can't escape the longing for home."

For most of my mid- to late teens and all my adult life we were decidedly not close. In my memory more often than not my treks as a young boy down the rails to the wooden trestle over Sugar Creek, and my wanderlust for following the Penn Central line to somewhere else, were connected to my father and some hurt, anger, or disappointment, real or imagined, within that relationship.

For a time when I was in my thirties the distance between us widened to something like a chasm: the disparity between my hopes for the relationship and the reality I experienced in it; the desire for consistency, predictability, and presence in my life and the lives of my two children, and what I perceived to be the opposite with him. Throughout that time and despite the chasm, I tried to act on the Bible's admonition to honor my father. I did so by consistently naming the three gifts he placed in my life: the love of baseball, the centrality of music in our family's life, and the gift of my first guitar when he brought home for me, a sickly child, a kid-sized red and white electric instrument and amplifier, along with a beginner's songbook, from which I learned to play pop tunes of the day such as "Wild World," "Peace Train," and "You've Got a Friend." In later years I did it by phoning him weekly on my commutes home from work, listening as he gave updates on the shows he'd been watching, the results of his favorite football and college basketball teams' most recent games, and how he was feeling physically at that time.

Small but consistent gestures. And then, suddenly, even those ended.

On a frigid December morning at St. Francis Hospital, my father lay in the cardiac intensive care unit. Monitors buzzed and pinged and signaled something significant was happening after hours of utterly no change. The nurse on duty walked in and calmly said, "It's happening," and unplugged the power cord from the wall.

"He's gone," she said somberly, stepping back from the bed.

He had died after four days of his family—four children and our mother—keeping vigil at his bedside. He never regained consciousness from a stroke. But literally in the instant we heard the words "he's gone," a Brahms lullaby played over the St. Francis Hospital sound system, signaling a newborn child had just entered the world in a nearby maternity ward. I looked at my brother, Darren, standing next to me and asked, "Did you hear that?"

It was a moment of grace, the symmetry of death and new life, of lost and found. It was a moment of gravity, knowing that our father, at seventy-nine years of age, would no longer be present to cajole, fuss, or watch a ballgame with. It was a final recognition that the longed-for textures of a father and son relationship would never come to pass—a closeness, a mutual investment in each other, the creation of new memories together. And it was a moment of recognizing the reality of the aging process I didn't fully see in the whirlwind that makes up our daily existence.

"Home is a place that one is born into, that grounds our souls to that home that is with us wherever we are and that we can never separate from," my Argentina-based missionary friend has said. "That home of ten thousand things. That home that *is* us. Within us. Connects us. In widening circles outward, as we learn to live and love and discover we are always, always, just walking each other home."

As the nurse's voice quietly declared that my dad had died, I wondered, "Is this restless, wandering soul finally at home?" I hoped so, for him.

And one day, for me, as well.

~

It was a hot August day when I left my suburban home and drove four hours to the rural farm of a family member during a particularly challenging season. After a late meal and a hike through the forty acres of land she owned, with the sun fully set in the western sky and a shimmering canopy of stars above, my two hiking companions and I walked east on the black-topped country road. The darkness, created by the total absence of light pollution I have come to know in my Chicago-area village, was arresting. The darkness and the silence were mesmerizing.

But even more so it was the fireflies.

They literally filled the meadow on one side of the road and the woodlands on the other, sparkling, shining, dancing, and beckoning as they lit up the sky with their yellow-green pulsing, silent rhythms. We continued to walk in silence, peering left and then right as the fireflies seemingly said to us, "There is light in this dark world!" It was a dazzling show put on by the natural world in a way I'd never seen before—or, at least, not as an adult. I am prone to melancholy, to seeing the glass half empty. That night, my cup was overflowing with joy as I walked and watched.

The wonder of childhood, running after fireflies with a Ball jar in hand, holes poked in the lid, came to me as if it were yesterday, and not five and a half decades ago, and it was strangely comforting. It was an odd and peaceful sense of home. In my mind, I began to hum the melody from a Paul Simon song from my childhood—a song written for *his* infant son—that spoke in reassuring words about fireflies flashing, the bearing of light, and the knowledge that everything would be alright, so I could close my weary eyes and rest. It was a reminder of the now and the not-yet home. It was a whisper of God's care in the midst of my longing for home.

The Longing for Home
A Playlist

"My Little Town," Simon & Garfunkel, from the recording *The Best of Simon & Garfunkel* (1999)

"Longing for Home," Cherish the Ladies, from the recording *Country Crossroads* (2011)

"Railwalker," Brooks Williams, from the recording *How the Nighttime Sings* (1991)

"Home," Rich Mullins, from the recording *Winds of Heaven, Stuff of Earth* (1988)

"St. Judy's Comet," Kenny Loggins, from the recording *Return to Pooh Corner* (1994)

"Home," Jack Johnson, from the recording *From Here to Now to You* (2013)

CHAPTER 2

The Longing for an Undivided Life

> Only when the pain of our dividedness becomes more than we can bear do most of us embark on an inner journey toward living "divided no more."
>
> **Parker Palmer, *A Hidden Wholeness***

The town of Green Lake, Wisconsin, boasts twenty-seven miles of shoreline around what is touted as the area's deepest inland lake. It's a state proudly known for equal emphasis on agriculture, recreation, and industry *and* for its state mascot Bucky, a badger with a fierce scowl on its face and a red- and white-striped sweater emblazoned with a large *W* wrapped around its puffed-up chest.

On a frigid early spring day, with ice encrusting the shallow edges of the lake and frost on the window panes of our rooms overlooking it, a group of twenty people gathered at a retreat center in Green Lake near the Roger Williams Inn, established in 1930 and named after the English Protestant theologian (1603–1688), an early proponent of religious freedom and separation of church and state.

Our group, comprising people drawn from throughout the United States and places as distant as Argentina, had come to Green Lake not to delve into the issues that concerned Williams centuries ago. Rather, we were interested in a different kind of freedom—the freedom of an undivided life. We were individually and collectively looking for pathways to that freedom.

I most certainly longed for that.

Our guide over the course of three days was the author, activist, and education theorist Parker Palmer, who has devoted much of his career to helping people bring a congruence between their inner and outer lives, even as he has authentically wrestled with maintaining the same in his own experience, often publicly relaying the challenges in his books, recordings, teaching, and interviews. Years earlier I had met Palmer, spending an enjoyable summer afternoon sipping iced tea and sharing a meal on his back porch as we talked about his book *On the Brink of Everything: Grace, Gravity and Getting Old.* I was the journalist posing questions and listening as he joyfully, thoughtfully answered, regularly pausing his remarks to ask me about my life, work, family, and perspective on any number of subjects that arose in our conversation. It was a somewhat uncharacteristic and decidedly endearing contrast to many other people I have interviewed over the course of my career.

That conversation, borne out of a long-held appreciation for Palmer's books, had an effect well beyond the articles that emerged out of it. Far more importantly, it was a catalyst for coming in touch more fully with my own longing for an undivided self and for attempting to bring greater congruity between my inner and outer life.

A powerful line from Palmer's book *A Hidden Wholeness* remained with me on that journey: "We arrive in this world undivided, integral, whole," he wrote. "But sooner or later, we erect a wall between our inner and outer lives, trying to protect what is within us or to deceive the people around us. Only when the pain of our dividedness becomes more than we can bear do most of us embark on an inner journey toward living 'divided no more.'"

From the first time I read those words to well beyond the time I drove several hours back to my home after spending that day with him, those words rang true, as I reflected on our conversation and the stirrings of my soul related to several dimensions of dividedness, including my work, my experience of church, and persistent questions about my public persona and my private self-conception.

That meeting was a prompt to learn more and to dive deeper into an awareness of the markings and makings of undivided life. To embark on a journey toward more consistent, life-giving integration is a challenge. Yet the conversation and those words that leaped off the printed page merged to become a catalyst to deal with the walls of division that too often were present in my life, the places of dis-integration I knew were within me, and longed to see healed. What also merged in that quest was a nudge to invite God to meet me there and to show me a way forward.

Now, on the shores of Green Lake, I was a part of a small circle of people who joined together, listened, spoke vulnerably, journaled, prayed in solitude, and considered steps toward integration, toward an undivided life.

Among the questions we wrestled with in pairs, in the larger group, and on our own with journals in hand were, "What is the root of our loss of integration that we once had? How did the division happen? And what is our path to reintegration?"

Theological constructs such as original sin and original blessing, among other adjacent topics that may or may not be related to an integrated life, have bedeviled religious discourse for centuries. Sometimes starting with less discourse is helpful.

I find children are instructive when contemplating our longing for an undivided life. These days, I have the joy of sharing significant portions of my life with six grandchildren, ages five to twelve. Though I have a role in teaching them and offering stories and wisdom from a long life filled with joy and sorrow, victory and failure, faithfulness and stumbling, it's equally true that they are *my* teachers as well.

Spending time with young children is an exercise in viewing integrated, undivided lives. With young children you see unfiltered, unmasked persons: wonder, joy, exuberance, unrestrained inquisitiveness, ever-present self-preoccupation, a belief that they are good at whatever they set their mind to, out-front anger, persistent selfishness, heartfelt tears. It's all there in living color.

As we age, however, through the impact of our families, the education and other systems, our churches, workplaces, our pursuit of success and stature, something forms that separates us from our true selves—a mismatch of deep-rooted temperament and environment, or some combination of these and other dimensions of our lives. We begin to build a wall between how we present ourselves and who we are in the truest of our true selves. We learn to project what we learn (or believe) is expected of us. We deceive ourselves and others out of some desire for perceived self-protection. We don masks because we don't like what we see in the mirror.

Our ability to receive love and acceptance from others and to live consistently in the light of the assurance of God's grace leads us to be like river water stirred up by storms, in need of allowing sediment to settle, to be still and at peace. Even high-achieving individuals are prone to experiencing that particular shame known as "imposter phenomenon," an intense and persistent belief that one's success isn't deserved or wasn't arrived at via legitimate means despite the documented evidence of success over a long period of time.

What emerges is a dissonance between our core beliefs and values on the one hand and our actions on the other. Between the once-held idea that God loves and accepts us as we are and the "self-hatred," as Brennan Manning put it, of the person we believe we actually are. Our integrity is strained, compromised, hit and miss, challenged.

If those descriptions feel familiar to you, know that you are not alone. They are familiar to me as well, and to most of us—and are an invitation to consider how we might move toward the call to an undivided life.

~

The manifestations of a divided life are as varied as the people who inhabit the planet, unique to our individual experience of the world and the soil of our interior lives. But in my experience, I have noted a number of classic signals of dis-integration that serve as something akin to a tornado or hurricane siren imploring me to take shelter before the storm hits. When I have recognized these siren sounds, tending to them through both solitude and community, I have gained equilibrium. When I have ignored the signals, I sense a flywheel of dis-integration gaining momentum that eventually leads to a desire to fight or to flee, a sense of desolation rather than consolation. Your dis-integration list will likely be different from mine, but the following loudly sound the siren:

- Unending busyness or its opposite, lethargy
- Exhaustion
- Situational depression
- A hurried and harried life
- Endless ruminating on words I've said and others left unsaid, how the words I've spoken were received
- Continual fear of being less than what is expected of me by some mysterious "other"
- A sense of not measuring up to some mysterious standard

- A fear of being considered a fraud
- Defensiveness in response to understandable questions or reasonable suggestions
- The absence of patience, kindness, and gentleness
- A fear of disappointing God

When these signals, among others, appear and I am alert to them and willing to attend to them, the gap between the inner and outer life heals and regenerates. When I avoid the signals' sounds, I put another brick on the wall.

The cost of a divided life, Palmer warns, is high:

> I pay a steep price when I live a divided life—feeling fraudulent, anxious about being found out, and depressed by the fact that I am denying my own selfhood. The people around me pay a price as well, for now they walk on ground made unstable by my dividedness. How can I affirm another's identity when I deny my own? How can I trust another's integrity when I defy my own? A fault line runs down the middle of my life, and whenever it cracks open—divorcing my words and actions from the truth I hold within—things around me get shaky and start to fall apart.

As the gathering revealed both the fault lines and the ways I understood healing the divide might come, I began to understand that spiritual direction is one of the key routes back to integration. The quiet, consistent, caring attention to what God may be saying in my life made possible by the helpful presence of another trusted person is a way God meets me most significantly in this longing. The questions the director poses in response to my own words have helped me consider what God may be saying to me, what God may want me to be attentive to. It connects threads of my inner narratives about dis-integration and asks if there are other ways to view those stories.

~

As we gathered on the second day of our three-day retreat, we were asked to create something like a Möbius strip, named after the German mathematician and astronomer August Ferdinand Möbius (1790–1868).

We were given a slim horizontal strip of paper and on one side asked to write characteristics of our outer or "onstage" life. That is, what we project or desire for others to see. On the other side of the strip, we were to write about our inner or "backstage" life, how we view ourselves, who we are when no one is looking. Ultimately, we grasped each end of the horizontal strip and did a one-half turn and suddenly the onstage and backstage were all meshed together. There was no inner or outer. There was a decided unity.

Palmer writes, "The mechanics of the Möbius strip are mysterious, but its message is clear: whatever is inside us continually flows outward to help form, or deform, the world—and whatever is outside us continually flows inward to help form, or deform, our lives. The Möbius strip is like life itself: here, ultimately, there is only one reality."

In a time before the Möbius strip, I remember driving along an interstate freeway on a trip to interview a well-known Christian author. As I drove, I listened for the first time to an audio recording by Brennan Manning, the author of a number of classic works of spirituality including *The Ragamuffin Gospel* and *Abba's Child*. The recording, from a speech he gave in Indianapolis, was titled "Healing Our Image of God and Ourselves." As I drove and listened, I encountered the words, "My friends, I believe that Christianity happens when men and women experience the reckless, raging confidence that comes from knowing, from experiencing the God of Jesus Christ. With this God, there is no need to be wary, and no need to be afraid."

Manning repeatedly and passionately spoke of the relentless tenderness and altogether reliable love of Christ in that recording. And he spoke about people who live with a constant fear and preoccupation with the acceptance and approval of others and of God.

He spoke as if to me that day. Not just people *like* me but *me*.

I have a distinct memory of pulling to the side of the interstate freeway as I heard those words in order to wipe the uncontrollable tears from my eyes and compose myself emotionally enough to finish the drive. Not since reading the "Grand Inquisitor" section of Fyodor Dostoyevsky's novel *The Brothers Karamazov* many years before had I been so profoundly and immediately shaken by someone's spoken or written words.

The longing within myself to not only be seen, be understood, to reassemble a life that felt like it was all separate puzzle parts, was a life-changing moment, opening me up to a new way of viewing the image I carried of both God and of myself. And it was a moment that ultimately led me to the group in Wisconsin.

"I believe Jesus calls all of us to let go of the desire to appear good," wrote Manning in one of his early books, "to give up the appearance of being good, so that we can listen to the word within us and move in the mystery of who we are. The preoccupation with projecting the perfect image, of being a model Christian and edifying others with our virtues, leads to self-consciousness, sticky pedestal behavior, and bondage to human respect."

Manning was no pious, buttoned-down-life person. He didn't pretend to have his life together, nor did he keep up appearances. In many ways he was, instead, very childlike, a "what you see is what you get" person, with a message "for the inconsistent, unsteady disciples whose cheese is falling off their cracker" and "earthen vessels who shuffle along on feet of clay."

As I returned from that trip to Chicago, I felt something of the Emmaus road—a longing for voices like Manning's to guide me, to gently, humbly, and powerfully remind me I am a trustworthy Abba's beloved child.

Other voices and mentors came to guide me in this longing for an integrated life, among them the late Henri Nouwen, who wrote and spoke about the subject with unceasing vulnerability throughout his career.

He once wrote, "In the midst of this world the Son of God, Jesus Christ, appears and offers us new life, the life of the Spirit of God. We desire this life, but we also realize it is so radically different from what we are used to that even aspiring to it seems unrealistic."

Person after person began to address this longing within me. As Manning assured listeners they are beloved of God, Nouwen asked how human persons can move toward unity within themselves, a struggle he himself lived into and wrote about powerfully in many of his books. Ultimately, it's the work of God's Spirit that does the re-creation, he says, but the longing is met in daily spending time "in the presence of God when we can listen to his voice precisely in the midst of our many concerns. It also calls for the persistent endeavor to be with others in a new way by seeing them not as people to whom we can cling in fear, but as fellow human beings with whom we can create new space for God."

His three-pronged approach—committing to solitude and silence in the presence of God, being in community with others, and the guidance of a spiritual director—as the primary means of bringing unity and integration has been a siren response and has been echoed by other devotional masters through the centuries. The approach has been the primary means God has addressed and met me in this longing of the heart. And something Parker Palmer's Center for Courage and Renewal emphasizes is what it calls "the courage way" approach, which integrates both solitude and community, and allows for an understanding of the cycles and seasons of

life, with the calling to hold an understanding of the both/
and—rather than either/or polarities.

~

Not long ago I crossed the threshold of my sixtieth year, an
age that I once looked upon as being very *old*—but no longer
do. And yet that marker has caused me to think more deeply
about the years I have remaining on the planet and what I
would like to see become ever truer of my life as the years
increase. Principally, I long to be able to say and to *know* that
I have been present in this world—present to my family, my
friendships, my work; present to the needs of the community
I am a part of—and that such presence was borne out of my
true self. I long to be able to say and to *know* that I have been
present to God's voice in my soul, and have responded more
often than not to God's promptings. I long to have been present with the gifts I have been given by a loving God, which
have been nurtured by many people around me even in the
midst of the sufferings and stumbling that are a part of what
it means to be human.

~

On the last of the three days spent along the shores of Green
Lake in east central Wisconsin, we retreatants were each
handed an envelope and loose-leaf sheets of paper. After a
brief word of instruction from the retreat leader, we scattered

throughout the property to tackle our reflective assignment, utter quiet descending as we went. Some walked to the Roger Williams Inn, others to benches in a still-flowerless sunken garden showing the wear and tear of an Upper Midwest winter. Some fanned out to the shores of the lake, while others took up residence, pen and paper in hand, at picnic tables dotting the landscape.

Wherever we went, our task was the same: to write a letter to ourselves articulating our growing edge as people, our longing for an undivided life, and our planned steps to achieve that with the help of God's Spirit. We were writing down the words, the sense of wholeness we wanted to take away with us as we returned to our homes. We were reminding ourselves what we experienced during this time set apart for both community and solitude.

When we regathered to say goodbye, we sealed the envelopes, addressed them to ourselves, and handed them back to the person who had led us through three days of teaching, conversation, and self-examination.

In one of his classic works, the theologian Karl Barth wrote, "Grace and gratitude belong together like heaven and earth. Grace evokes gratitude like the voice of an echo. Gratitude follows grace like thunder lightning." I have always loved the connection he made between the grace of God extended to us, and our response of gratitude.

Six months after handing over the note to myself, with summer beginning to recede and autumn just over the horizon, the letter arrived in my mailbox. I slid it open, pulled out the paper, and sat down to read words I had written to myself on that cold spring morning. I reread the stories I'd written about movements I desired to make along a continuum:

- A move from concern with what others thought about me to acting out of my true self
- A shift from a spirit of fear to a sense of courage
- A change from needing to be right to wanting to listen, hear, and understand another's perspective
- A shift from performance to resting, trusting, being

They were words I needed to remember, stories of what I'd learned during those days in Green Lake.

Gratitude, following grace. Hope for an undivided life in the present and the future. Thanks be to God.

The Longing for an Undivided Life
A Playlist

"Lullaby to Eternity," Alice Sara Ott, from
the recording *Echoes of Life* (2021)

"The Lord's Prayer," Larry Carlton, from
the recording *Alone/Never Alone* (1986)

"My Peace," the Taizé Community, from
the recording *Songs of Taizé* (1999)

"Earth, Water, Wind, Fire," the Belfast Harp
Orchestra, from the recording *Celtic Harpestry* (1998)

"Writing a Better Story," Carrie Newcomer,
from the recording *The Point of Arrival* (2019)

"Safe Harbor," Richard Souther, from
the recording *Cross Currents* (1989)

CHAPTER 3

The Longing for Freedom
from Fear and Anxiety

But all the while, there was one thing we most needed
even from the start, and certainly will need from here
on out into the New Jerusalem: the ability to take our
freedom seriously and act on it, to live not in fear of
mistakes but in the knowledge that no mistake can
hold a candle to the love that draws us home.

Robert Farrar Capon, *Between Noon and Three*

I t hit like a thunderbolt from the heavens without a moment
of warning, as these things almost by clinical definition do.
And it came not in solitude, but in the middle of a massive
crowd of people.

Twenty thousand booksellers, authors, agents, and media
had gathered at the sprawling Jacob Javits Center in New York
City for the 1989 installment of the American Booksellers

Association's (ABA) annual convention, at that time the largest gathering of its kind in an English-speaking country.

The 1989 convention showcased new books for that fall season by well-known writers of the day including James A. Michener, Stephen King, Tom Clancy, Erma Bombeck, the Rev. Andrew M. Greeley, Leo Buscaglia, Robert Fulgham, and Pulitzer Prize–winning journalist Ellen Goodman, whose collection of syndicated columns were to be published that autumn under the title *Making Sense*.

Doonesbury cartoonist Garry B. Trudeau, mystery writer John le Carré, and Italian novelist, philosopher, and social critic Umberto Eco were among the hundreds of authors who appeared in person, as did former US First Lady Nancy Reagan, who had left the White House that January along with her two-term husband, President Ronald Reagan.

But on that Saturday evening in June, I was listening to a psychiatrist, teacher, and spiritual director from the Shalem Institute, Gerald G. May, speak on his then new book *Addiction and Grace: Love and Spirituality in the Healing of Addictions* when the thunderbolt struck.

A panic attack.

I remember relatively few details of that night, but I do recall that in almost an instant I began to sense the walls of the cavernous hotel ballroom closing in on me with increasing velocity. There was a simultaneous racing of my heart such as I'd never experienced, and a sensation of my face being on fire. I looked at my wife of six years seated next to me and simply said, "*I have to get out of here.*"

We hurriedly left the room without saying goodbye to bookseller friends sitting at our table, elegant wine glasses in hand and looks of confusion on their faces. We hailed a taxi in a steady stream of rain and made our way to our third-tier hotel room, where I collapsed into bed in what I recall as something akin to a catatonic stupor, with a decidedly large dose of shame.

Despite Cindy's caring persistence, I was unable to articulate that night what had happened other than to say, "The walls were closing in. I had to leave."

As the sun rose the next morning, the two of us abandoned our book-buying responsibilities at the Javits Center and boarded a ferry for Ellis Island and the Statue of Liberty. Later, we had a luncheon somewhere in lower Manhattan in the shadow of the World Trade Center towers, where we talked about the night before and haltingly, quietly explored the possible answers to the questions, "*What happened? And why?*"

I remember purchasing a copy of John Lennon's seminal album *Imagine* from a nearby music store to listen to on a Sony Walkman, somehow sensing that his anthem celebrating the absence of *both* heaven *and* hell and the presence of only sky above would be strangely comforting to my state of mind.

It took me some time to connect the panic attack and its intense fear and anxiety that night to the convergence of Gerald May's topic of addiction and grace, the prevalence of multiple generations of alcohol abuse in my family system, and the room filled with people merrily lifting glasses as they listened to the speaker. Had I not gotten out of the room, I fear I would have bellowed out, *"Aren't you listening to this man speak on addictions?"* and, in doing so, utterly embarrassed myself.

Clearly, I had a lot of internal work to do.

It was the first and the most intense attack of its kind I've ever had, but it would not be the last. It instilled in me a longing to be free of whatever was at root and a deep desire to understand how to manage the anxiety when it happened. It also gave me empathy for others who struggle with the overlooked and misunderstood topic of mental health, perhaps especially within the context of the church.

~

In the same way we might consider pain we experience as a gift—a warning of impending danger—fear serves a good purpose in our lives. As children, our parents would offer instructions about the dangers of stovetop heat, jumping into deep water without an adult present, getting in a car with someone we did not know, or failing to look both ways before we crossed the street. As teenagers, we would hear admonitions about careful, focused, and sober driving, about choosing our friends wisely, and not being out too late—all guidance borne out of known or reasonable fears about the outcomes if we chose otherwise.

Psychiatrists suggest that fear and anxiety often overlap but have distinctive characteristics. Fear relates to a known or understood threat, whereas anxiety is "a diffuse, unpleasant, vague sense of apprehension." A panic attack, in my experience, is anxiety on overdrive.

Margaret Wehrenberg, a licensed psychologist in private practice and the author of a number of books on anxiety and depression, suggests that the occurrence of anxiety like I had that night in New York is without question pervasive in North America, and I suspect it's true for many other cultures around the world as well. She cites a statistic from the Anxiety Disorder Association of America that says 40 million Americans will experience a panic attack during their lifetime.

For each of those 40 million people there is a complex and unique web of reasons for the intense panic, anxiety, and unhealthy fear we carry with us. Depression, brain chemistry, families of origin, abuse, unresolved guilt, biology, rejection, and more may contribute to our experiences. However, I believe a common desire lives within those of us who find its presence all too familiar.

We long to be free from debilitating anxiety and fear in order to enter fully into relationships, our work, and opportunities that lie before us. At times, those of us who experience this type of anxiety and fear have difficulty understanding where it comes from or what to do about it. Therapy, spiritual direction, and vulnerable friendships have all been sources of strength.

As have trusted voices in books.

Among the spiritual voices who have understood anxiety, sharing a private wrestling in a public way through his writing, was Howard Thurman, former chaplain of both Howard

University and Boston University. In his enduring book *Meditations of the Heart*, Thurman writes,

> God is present with me in the midst of my anxieties. I affirm in my own heart and mind the reality of His presence. He makes immediately available to me the strength of His goodness, His courage. My anxieties are real; they are the result of a wide variety of experiences, some of which I understand, some of which I do not understand. One thing I know concerning anxieties: they are real to me. Sometimes they seem more real than the presence of God. When this happens, they dominate my mood and possess my thoughts. The presence of God does not always deliver me from anxiety, but it always delivers me from anxieties. Little by little, I am beginning to understand that deliverance from anxiety means fundamental growth in spiritual character and awareness. It becomes a quality of being, emerging from deep within, giving to all the dimensions of experience a vast immunity against being anxious. A ground of calm underlies experiences whatever may be the tempestuous character of events. This calm is the manifestation in life of the active, dynamic Presence of God.

There are so many things to appreciate in Thurman's brief meditation, especially for those of us who have lived with panic attacks, intense fears, or anxieties: his bedrock assurance that God is present in the midst of the anxiety we feel. His certainty that God makes available to us God's own courage. The bold declaration that whatever anyone else may think about them, the anxieties we feel are real to us. His belief that there is a "ground of calm" underlying our experiences, regardless of the particulars of our episodes. Reassuring words such as Thurman's are one of the ways God has met me in the midst of this longing of the heart.

As are repeated assurances in the Bible.

One of the most common refrains in Scripture is the simple admonition, "Be not afraid." Nearly one hundred uses of that phrase are found from Genesis to Zechariah in the Old Testament, and from Matthew to Revelation in the New Testament. Deuterocanonical books such as Tobit, Judith, Sirach, Maccabees, and Esdras, likewise contain passages exhorting their hearers and readers to "be not afraid" or "fear not." The repetition throughout Scripture and within its individual portions suggests to me it's something that invites our attention and seeks our response.

In part, through it being set to a song by Roby Duke titled "O, Magnify the Lord," one of the early portions of Scripture I memorized is Psalm 34, a psalm of praise for deliverance from trouble. When King David felt threatened, he feigned madness before Abimelech, the king of Shechem and the son of the biblical judge Gideon. David's behavior, borne out of his fears, drove Abimelech away. In the psalm, we read David's words, "I sought the Lord, and he answered me, and delivered me from all my fears."

As our longing deepens we ask, "What is our path to such deliverance?"

~

As much as any writer I've encountered, it has been the late Henri Nouwen who has tutored me in this area. Nouwen's writings have a level of vulnerability that is at once disarming and instructive, and they have become a mirror for my own soul. Through them I am reminded that my fears and anxieties are real, have been shared by others, and can be healed.

"We are called—we are urged—to bring our pain into the healing presence of the cross," Nouwen writes in *Following Jesus: Finding Our Way Home in an Age of Anxiety*, a book crafted out of a series of lectures he delivered during Lent in 1985 at a church in Cambridge, Massachusetts. "[We] pray, 'Lord, I am so fearful today. I don't know where it comes from, but I am anxious and fearful. It is there, Lord, I want to bring it into your presence and bring it right into the Garden of Gethsemane and connect it with your anguish so that my fear becomes your struggle. The struggle to live.'"

As I have reflected and journaled on my seasons of fear and anxiety and a desire to find freedom in the midst of them, I've noted being met through the care of counselors, spiritual directors, and deep spiritual friendships. But God has also met me in the midst of this longing through solitude, silence, and praying at the stations of the cross.

~

It was at a silent retreat at a monastery where I was first exposed to the practice of walking the stations of the cross in silence, reflecting on fourteen specific settings of Christ, from the garden of Gethsemane to Christ's being placed in a tomb. It was an unrushed, reflective exercise that prior to that time was foreign to my experience, and something about it cracked open my heart to see Christ's presence in my own pain, loneliness, anxiety, fear.

Carmen Acevedo Butcher has likened the stations of the cross to places where we stop and be still, "waiting for a bus, taxi, or train, in transit to somewhere else." She continues, "Similarly, in this life we are always waiting on God, en route to heaven." Stopping before each work of art depicting familiar biblical passages, the reality of Christ's companionship with me in the midst of anxiety came alive in fresh, deep, and enduring ways. I have returned to that exercise on a number of occasions, including a poignant gathering with my long-term colleagues, and the waiting at those stations has continued to bring light and life.

It has been my experience that when I have made space for God to speak in solitude and silence and through prayer, my fears and anxieties are most often allayed, and peace found, something spirituality writer Ruth Haley Barton contends as well: solitude and silence are the fertile soil in which all other Christian disciplines (or practices) are planted.

For years, I had significant anxiety about speaking in public. My body would literally break out in red blotches, my voice would quaver, and my hands would tremble, at times uncontrollably. And yet as a young adult I increasingly found myself in roles within the church or in business settings where I was expected to do the *very* thing that paralyzed me with fear and anxiety. As the expectations grew, I sought to meet them by developing a prayer ritual leading up to those speaking occasions. I would focus on the people who were on the receiving end of my words, asking that God would allow nothing I said to detract or harm, and that something—even if only *one* thing—I said would contribute to their well-being, their hopefulness, their understanding. This decentering (moving from being mindful primarily of my own anxiety to a focus on the receivers' well-being) enabled me to largely overcome this unhealthy mental and physiological state.

While I still don't enjoy public speaking, thankfully, it no longer incapacitates me.

Similarly, airline travel brought an intense experience of anxiety and impacted my work for an extended period of time, even as my job required much more travel than ever before. The fear grew from an incident that took place in the waning days of Colorado's Stapleton International Airport in 1994. A Continental Airlines flight I was on from Indianapolis to Denver, a Boeing 737, was directed by air traffic control to make an approach for its landing at the same time and on the same runway that another aircraft was positioned for takeoff. Everyone was jolted by the last-second aborted landing, even as the pilot, circling the city and beginning our approach for a second time, apologized for the unusual maneuver he had undertaken, acknowledging what happened in a voice that said, without words, "Wow, that was *way* too close!"

For years afterward, my increasingly frequent domestic and international flights for my work were the source of intense anxiety. As with the public speaking and other challenges I continued to meet, it was a prayer mechanism I developed after boarding that allowed me to focus on the well-being of other passengers, the crew, and yes, myself throughout each takeoff and landing, the two portions of flight that, research suggests, are most dangerous. I also developed a habit of reading a passage of Scripture or reciting the lyrics of a song that supported me deep within to "be not afraid." It became something of a liturgy, those practices. And each one I received as a lifeline.

~

One of the ways God has consistently met me in the midst of fear and anxiety, whatever its forms or reasons, is through recorded music. Just as the concept of *saudade* in Portuguese-speaking cultures is most readily expressed through music, I have found companions for calming fear and anxiety through the art of songwriters, church hymnody, and times of contemplation and meditation on musical words, melodies, and structures.

I'm not alone. For millennia, Jewish and Christian spiritual tradition has looked to the Psalms, the Scriptures set to music, for hope, courage, calm, and for understanding and engaging the emotional landscape of our lives.

During sleep-deprived nights, it is not uncommon for me to "hear" songs rooted in the Psalms, in particular, filling my mind and bringing a sense of calm. Or liturgical works such as Robert J. Dufford, SJ's "Be Not Afraid," whose words offer companionship:

> Be not afraid.
> I go before you always.
> Come follow me,
> and I will give you rest.

Songs such as Dufford's act as a reminder of God's presence in the midst of fear and anxiety. For me, they act as touchstones.

"Next to the Word of God," wrote the church reformer Martin Luther, "music deserves the highest praise." In the liturgy or on the airplane, I've experienced music as a companion regardless of the season: In times of joy and wonder, sadness and grief, exhilaration and hope. But especially in times of fearfulness and anxiousness.

~

Another way God has met me in this longing is with the practice of St. Ignatius of Loyola's daily examen, which I first discovered not through exposure from the church but rather by putting into practice the very books I published as part of my work. On long walks at the end of a work day and sometimes at midday I would quietly reflect on the people or events that had brought life, light, or hope and offer prayers of thanksgiving for those. Conversely, I would reflect on and name the people or events or situations that were connected to frustration, sorrow, or darkness, and ask for God's help. Later, I began to journal in response to this practice and to look for recurring themes, situations, and people who populated the desolations and consolations.

A Spanish priest who lived from 1491 to 1556, Ignatius founded the Society of Jesus (the Jesuits), an order whose members have included influential people from a variety of academic disciplines and religious traditions, including the poet Gerard Manley Hopkins, the writer Anthony de Mello, the scientist Georges Lemaître, and Francis, the first Jesuit pope. However, Ignatius is best known for the spiritual exercises he wrote to spiritually companion people through their lives. The spiritual exercises, one of which is the daily examen, are practiced to this day by people throughout the world.

As Adele Calhoun noted in her book *Spiritual Disciplines Handbook*, Ignatius wrote the examen for a portion of the order so that they would know how to detect the movement of God in their lives.

In the most basic expression of Ignatius's daily examen practice that I have received and utilized, those who live the practice are encouraged at the end of each day to set aside time to ask ourselves about and reflect on what are called the desolations and consolations we experienced in that particular day. In the examen, we ask ourselves questions like the following:

> Where have we felt a deep connection to God?
> Where have we felt God's absence?
> What in the day was life-giving?
> What was life-thwarting or depleting?
> What is this telling us?

For myself and so many others, journaling responses to these reflective questions is a pathway of hope, healing, and recentering, especially in the midst of an anxious season.

"A person dwells in a state of consolation when she or he is moving toward God's active presence in the world," writes author Vinita Hampton Wright. "We know we are moving in this way when we sense the growth of love or faith or mercy or hope—or any qualities we know as gifts of the Holy Spirit."

By contrast, Wright says, "a person dwells in a state of desolation when she or he is moving away from God's active presence in the world. We know we are moving in this way when we sense the growth of resentment, ingratitude, selfishness, doubt, fear, and so on."

A lovely reframing of examen comes from Marilyn McEntyre, a writer whose varied works of poetry, art, list making, and spirituality I have long admired and benefited from. In her book *Where the Eye Alights*, she offers the simplicity of her five-step daily examen (often called the examination of conscience) that has been life-giving:

1. Become aware of God's presence.
2. Review the day with gratitude.
3. Pay attention to your emotions.
4. Choose one feature of the day and pray from it.
5. Look toward tomorrow.

"I love [the examen's] focus on gratitude, on how one has responded to guidance and presence, on particular moments,"

McEntyre writes. "It invites us always to remember that even in our 'erring and straying' we are held, witnessed, accompanied, and loved."

Among the aids for the examen pathway I have found helpful is one created by David Booram and Beth McLaughlin Booram, who operate the Fall Creek Abbey, an urban retreat center in Indianapolis. They have produced a set of cards with daily prompts that help us recognize where God is present and active in our days, reflect on what God's movement is stirring in us, and prayerfully, thoughtfully consider how we want to respond.

Whatever the particular mode you choose—or feel called to—the daily examen can be a helpful way of meeting God as we listen to our lives throughout seasons both joyful and anxious. The examen invites us to see God in the ordinary experiences, joys, and sorrows of our days. It can be a gateway to being attentive to other longings, including our yearning for an undivided self, forgiveness, and transformation. But for me, the examen has been particularly meaningful in the longing for freedom from fear and anxiety.

"The questions of the *examen* open our attention to how God's internal movement is present in our external comings and goings," writes Calhoun. "They lead us to listen deeply to the data of our lives. These questions help us pay attention to our mental state, our body responses, and our emotional baggage. The *examen* helps us recognize the things that bring us death and life. Once these things are known, they become part of our ongoing interaction with God in prayer."

~

The annual American Booksellers Association convention at the Jacob Javits Center ceased its operations in 2021, one of many victims of the changes to the way books garner exposure in our digital-driven world.

In the years since 1989, my work has continued to take me to New York City, the site of the first and most intense experience of debilitating anxiety. My son, four years old at that time, now works in a high-rise building a short distance from the ferry that takes vacationers off to Ellis Island and the Statue of Liberty, the places I journeyed for solace on that sunny June day so long ago when I began to try to answer the "What happened? And why?" questions.

Had I been able to stay in the booksellers ballroom that summer day in 1989, I might have heard Gerald G. May tell me something about my deepest longing and my most precious treasure, the thing that gives the most significant meaning to life—a desire for God, and an acceptance God's love of me. I might have heard May say,

Some of us have repressed this desire, burying it beneath so many other interests that we are completely unaware of it. Or we may experience it in different ways—as a longing for wholeness, completion, or fulfillment. Regardless of how we describe it, it is a longing for love. It is a hunger to love, to be loved, and to move closer to the Source of love. This yearning is the essence of the human spirit; it is the origin of our highest hopes and most noble dreams.

I couldn't hear his message that night, decades ago. Thankfully, I've heard it now. The daily examen, the Psalms set to music, and prayers both ancient and modern have been gateways to consolation, to being reminded that we are God's beloved.

I'm thankful for that as well.

The Longing for Freedom from Fear and Anxiety
A Playlist

"Be Not Afraid," John Michael Talbot, from
the recording *The Table of Plenty* (1997)

"Ubi Caritas," the Taizé Community, from
the recording *Taizé Instrumental 1* (2003)

"Worry Too Much," Mark Heard, from
the recording *Second Hand* (1991)

"O' Magnify the Lord," Roby Duke, from
the recording *Not the Same* (1982)

"Hold Me, Jesus," Rich Mullins, from the recording
A Liturgy, a Legacy, and a Ragamuffin Band (1993)

"Wrecking Ball," Jill Phillips, from the
recording *Writing on the Wall* (2005)

CHAPTER 4

The Longing for Forgiveness

Forgiving is love's revolution against life's unfairness. When we forgive, we ignore the normal laws that strap us to the natural law of getting even and, by the alchemy of love, we release ourselves from our own painful pasts.

Lewis B. Smedes, *Forgive and Forget*

G. C. Murphy five-and-dime stores served towns both large and small, primarily east of the Mississippi River and from the Canadian border to the Rio Grande. Throughout its four-generation history, the company was marked by ingenuity, family-like friendliness, and merchandising distinction.

The stores were founded by George Clinton Murphy in McKeesport, Pennsylvania, southeast of Pittsburgh. For more than eighty years, Murphy's five-and-dime stores connected people from all walks of life throughout the eastern and midwestern United States. In small mining towns in Appalachia, Murphy's (affordable) quality merchandise liberated residents from the tyranny of coal company-owned stores. In beach and resort towns from Delaware to Florida, Murphy's stores offered vacationers a place to find inexpensive souvenirs and staple items like coffee or cosmetics.

Before there were "fast-food" chains, Murphy's lunch counters in cities large and small united rich and poor, men and women, who needed a quick, cheap and filling 'bite to eat' before returning to the office or factory.

In his definitive history *For the Love of Murphy's: The Behind-the-Counter Story of a Great American Retailer*, Jason Togyer suggested that the company embodied many of the finest traditions of American entrepreneurship as it "weathered two world wars, a global depression, and several serious recessions."

The late folk musician, singer, and songwriter Nanci Griffith, in a spoken-word introduction to a live recording of the song "Love at the Five and Dime," talked about stores such as Woolworth, Kresge, and G. C. Murphy "smelling like popcorn and chewing gum rubbed around on the bottom of a leather-soled shoe."

Griffith got that right. The aroma is etched into the brains of long-time G. C. Murphy patrons, its wooden floors soaking in the smells of the popcorn machine, and what Togyer called "comfort food" served at the lunch counters.

But I have another reason to remember Murphy's—for an incident that placed an understanding of forgiveness and seeking it out squarely in my sights as a young person.

In my memory, G. C. Murphy stores had exceptional music departments with what looked to be an endless series of bins with the latest long-playing records and 45 RPMs—the iTunes singles of their day. It was that department that brought me to Murphy's anytime I had a ride there and a pocketful of coins earned in exchange for soda bottle returns at my local market. For an eleven-year-old boy wildly imagining himself to be a future singer-songwriter with a hit on one of those colorfully labeled records, G. C. Murphy's was *the* place to be.

It was in the Murphy's five-and-dime in Shelbyville, Indiana, that my earliest recollections of a longing for forgiveness are planted as a result of a poor decision, subsequent pangs of guilt, and misguided attempts to cleanse my conscience.

One chilly Saturday, my buddy Mike and I traveled with a family member about twenty miles into town to Murphy's to see what was new in the 45 record bins. As I rounded the corner, there it was: the object of my desire—Jim Croce's then-hit song "You Don't Mess Around with Jim."

The problem was that the record cost just a bit more than I had at my disposal.

Mike and I concocted a plan.

Nearby in what was commonly called a "discount cut-out" bin, I found a Neil Diamond 45 titled "Stones" that held some interest for me, just not nearly as much as Jim Croce's song. At its discounted price, even with a bit of tax, I had enough for that. I could buy the "Stones" 45 and get a paper bag. Then, I'd loop back by the rack that had "You Don't Mess Around with Jim" on it and discreetly slide it into my flat brown paper bag. Nobody would know. Nobody would be hurt.

Mike egged me on. I *really* wanted that Croce record.

I bought "Stones" and politely thanked the G. C. Murphy merchant, good citizen that I was. Then I walked back by the rack housing the new records for the fall of 1972 and slipped the Croce 45 into the bag and smugly strolled out of the store like Peter Lorre in Alfred Hitchcock's film *The Man Who Knew Too Much.*

My first and last foray into the dark world of retail theft had been completed.

I walked out to Mike's family member's pickup truck, and they dropped me off at my rural home some thirty minutes later. But before I ever got home, I felt a stab of guilt to a degree that I'd never remembered in the first eleven years of my life. And lest you think I had an overactive conscience from years sitting in the pews of a fire-and-brimstone church with a priest or pastor wagging a beefy "Shame on you!" finger in my face, the truth is that by then I'd stepped foot inside a place of worship only once in my life as far as I can recall.

The guilt came from elsewhere, something written on the human heart, on my heart. It was much later that I learned about what philosophers and theologians dating back to Aristotle have called "natural law."

When I dropped the phonograph needle down on the 45 to hear my very own copy of Jim Croce's record for the first time, the guilt intensified.

I'm unsure how long it took, but I do know that at some point I walked just a few minutes around the corner to the home of my friend Gayle, a fellow music lover with whom I traded 45 records, like others of that day who swapped Topps baseball cards. I was sure she would want "You Don't Mess Around with Jim," and, once out of my hands and home, the stains would be washed away and I could return to life as I'd always known it.

Approaching her, I asked, "Gayle, want to trade? I've got the latest from Jim Croce. What do you want to swap me for it?"

"Sorry, I already have it," she responded.

So, this is going to be harder than I imagined, this "cleansing" thing, I must have thought to myself as I trudged back home with the Croce 45 in hand.

A persistent youngster, I concocted yet another plan sometime later. Surely, I thought, if I just *bury* the Croce 45 and tell not a soul, that will take care of my transgression.

Why it didn't occur to me to simply confess my deed to my mom and ask her to drive me back to G. C. Murphy's and return the stolen record, I have no idea. Or why I didn't just toss it down the ravine toward the Penn Central railroad tracks where leaves, rusted beer and soda cans, and other debris would quickly cover it up, I've not a clue.

Instead, I found my father's shovel in the garage and went behind the house. Digging a hole about a foot deep and a bit wider than the circumference of a small record, I placed the material evidence of my crime—the copy of "You Don't Mess Around with Jim"—into the hole amid the dirt and clay and rocks. I pulled the topsoil back in place and tamped it down with my tennis shoes.

In my mind's eye as I retell the story all these years later, I hear the mournful strains of vocal and cello from the Beatles' "Eleanor Rigby" as Paul McCartney sings about a priest named Father McKenzie, who wiped the dirt from his hands and says, "No one was saved" before asking, "All the lonely people, where do they all come from?"

It was a defining moment—one I have obviously never forgotten—and I trace the longing for forgiveness and the beginning of my desire to understand it in all its complexities to that experience, though I have no doubt it was a subconscious longing at the time, not at all understood then as I understand it now.

It would be a few years before I embraced the forgiveness of God and far longer before I grappled with the multiple dimensions of forgiving and being forgiven by others—and forgiving ourselves. All of which I've experienced in powerful, life-giving ways. All of which are challenging to the human spirit.

But that experience, the theft of that record started me on a path of longing that I hardly understood at the time. The longing for a forgiveness that opens up our lives to receive and to extend grace and to build and maintain relationships. Its desolation—its absence—does the opposite, seeks to bury something that cannot be truly buried. It's a longing we share as human persons, even if we are inattentive to some aspects of it.

~

In the most radical of ways, through the person of Jesus, our longing for the forgiveness of God is met.

There's a rich passage from the Christian Scriptures, one theologians have parsed for centuries and heavy-handed evangelists are prone to use as a means of frightening people into change. But I love the simple and exuberant takeaway that the commentator in the *Renovaré Life with God Bible* offers in response to this passage:

> *By grace you have been saved.* Like a portrait beautifully framed, in a single sentence our best nouns are put on full display: "grace," "save," "faith." Take these words out of the Christian vocabulary, and our holidays have no celebration and the Blessed Sacrament itself is a child's tea party. The big realities of the Christian life are not things we wrestle from the hand of a parsimonious God; they are things God gives gladly with all the joy of a parent on Christmas morning.

What a lovely picture of the forgiveness and grace of God. And what a far superior pathway than attempting to bury transgressions in a backyard.

Just a few years after the G. C. Murphy incident, I was invited by Ann Myers, a woman in my small Indiana town, to attend a United Methodist summer camp, or what they, at the time and in the spirit of the great missiologist E. Stanley Jones, called a Christian ashram, in the southern part of the state. And it was there I first encountered words of Scripture that felt personal, and I heard of a pathway to the forgiveness of God.

The camp counselors handed out Living New Testaments to any attendees who (like me) didn't bring a Bible with them. Pieces of paper the size of business cards were given to us proclaiming "Jesus is Lord," "Jesus is the Way," and other mysterious phrases, utterly foreign to me. We were guided into reading passages from Romans, Ephesians, Colossians, and the Gospel of John, writings that couldn't have been more unfamiliar to my uninitiated heart and mind.

The co-ed gathering of teenagers would swim, canoe, and play athletic games during the day and attend tabernacle services at night, where the leaders of the camp would invite us to walk forward to "confess our sins and receive Christ." It was like hearing an entirely new and strange language—the music, the preaching, the exhortations to respond.

Night after night I stayed in my seat.

And yet it planted a seed, and I made some connection to my earlier awareness of the need for forgiveness. God was, like the lion Aslan in C. S. Lewis's *Chronicles of Narnia*, on the move. Connections came from so many places, including pop music of the day that *did* speak my language—George Harrison's "My Sweet Lord," Norman Greenbaum's "Spirit in the Sky," Cat Stevens's "The Wind," "Day by Day" from the musical *Godspell*, Sister Janet Mead's rendering of "The Lord's Prayer," and the Edwin Hawkins Singers' "Oh, Happy Day" among them.

Returning home, I joined the high school Campus Life gatherings, where the seed was watered. The seed grew through the reading of a now-long-forgotten book by Leslie Flynn titled *Me Be Like Jesus?* and it began to bear fruit in my undergraduate years of college. But the need to be tutored in the work of forgiveness in all its dimensions is a lifelong journey.

~

In his book *Forgiveness: Finding Peace through Letting Go*, Adam Hamilton, a United Methodist pastor, powerfully portrays the weight of guilt and shame that human persons carry. He describes ways we insert first a handful of pebbles, then small rocks, and finally large rocks into our backpacks. In the sermon series that formed the book, he showed the growing weight of the burden, adding the last stones before placing the whole load on his shoulders.

"I took my backpack, now filled with nearly sixty pounds of rocks," writes Hamilton, "hoisted it onto my back, and continued to preach and move around the chancel of the church. But quickly, I became winded. My shoulders drooped. One of my arms tingled, and my lower back hurt."

Hamilton compared the weight of the pack with the burdens we carry as a result of unrecognized and unresolved actions that "create an ever-widening gap between us and God, and our fellow human beings. They sap our joy and then our strength."

That weight is what I carried as I drove away from G. C. Murphy's on that winter day, though even as I felt it, I was unaware of what I was experiencing and what to do about it. In the grand scheme of a life's transgressions, stealing that record is merely symbolic of other pebbles, stones, and boulders I've carried at various junctures. Yet the stone gathering, when unresolved, saps joy and strength.

Among those things that release the stone-gathered weight is the weekly church liturgies where I am provided words and space for confession followed by a pronouncement of forgiveness. Like Adam Hamilton, I and the gathering of believers are all reminded to remove the backpack full of weight and place it on the altar of a God whose work is simultaneously already done and yet always ongoing. Rock removal.

~

Public defender and writer Jeanne Bishop lost her younger sister and brother-in-law when they were killed by a teenager in a break-in at her Chicago North Shore home in 1990. Through her book *Change of Heart*, Bishop's explorations of the subject of forgiving others carries a poignancy borne out of her loss. In her more recent book, *Grace from the Rubble*, Bishop portrays the unlikely friendship between Bill McVeigh, the father of Oklahoma City bomber Timothy McVeigh, and Bud Welch, whose only daughter, Julie, was among the 168 men, women, and children killed in the Alfred P. Murrah Federal Building on that devastating April morning in 1995.

"Forgiving someone means taking this thing you held on to—your heartbreak and hurt over a wrong someone has done—and letting it go with no guarantee of how it will all turn out," Bishop writes in *Grace from the Rubble.* "It's risky to be the one forgiven, too, because you know you have done nothing to earn or deserve it. Being forgiven is something we cannot do for ourselves; it must be given, a gift we know we cannot earn and can never truly repay."

The extension of forgiveness portrayed in both of Bishop's books is remarkable and a challenge to those of us who have endured far less harm in our own lives yet find it hard to forgive.

Few modern-era people I know of have spoken as powerfully into the topic of forgiveness as the late archbishop of South Africa and Nobel Peace Prize recipient Desmond Tutu. His chairmanship of the Truth and Reconciliation Commission (TRC) in his native country is but one example of his forgiveness work. Under his leadership, the TRC sought restorative (rather than punitive) justice in response to human rights abuses committed during apartheid. A three-fold approach guided the commission:

- Confession
- Forgiveness
- Restitution or making amends

Later in his life, in partnership with his daughter Mphoi, Tutu expanded on the subject of forgiveness and reconciliation that guided his work in South Africa and beyond in *The Book of*

Forgiving: The Fourfold Path for Healing Ourselves and Our World. When we endure hurt, harm, or loss, they write, we are faced with a choice of entering either a "revenge cycle" or a "forgiveness cycle" in response to our pain. The latter cycle, they say, is the one that brings healing to our own lives and to the world we inhabit. The fourfold path they suggest we walk down includes these concrete, actionable steps:

- Telling the story of what happened
- Naming the hurt that we feel
- Granting forgiveness as we recognize our shared humanity
- Renewing or releasing the relationship

"In the Truth and Reconciliation Commission, I saw over and over again how people courageously, nobly, magnificently chose the path of forgiveness," Tutu writes. "Any of those victims could have chosen to continue the cycle of violence and retaliation, but instead they chose to seek the truth, face their grief, and recognize both their own humanity and that of the perpetrators who had so grievously harmed them. They chose the difficult path of forgiveness. Forgiveness is rarely easy, but it is always possible."

The principles the Tutu's outline in *The Book of Forgiving* apply to issues the size of those addressed by the TRC—as well as what can at face value seem like much smaller, incidental concerns, such as one incident long after the G. C. Murphy's five-and-dime, in a bookstore whose product selection I was responsible for.

~

Rev. Jane was a joyful, radiant pastor of an African Methodist Episcopal Church from a nearby city, a longish drive from where my wife and I owned and operated a Christian bookstore in the 1980s. We enjoyed her frequent visits and serving both her and her congregation. Whenever she would come in, I smugly leaned on my sense of enlightenment and product choices, carrying books by and about civil rights leaders like Andrew Young, Ralph Abernathy, the Rev. Dr. Martin Luther King Jr., the liberation theologian James H. Cone, and Alex Haley's *The Autobiography of Malcolm X* on our shelves, not a common occurrence in similar shops specializing in Christian literature then or now.

But on one of her visits, Rev. Jane saw a product—a three-foot by five-foot Confederate flag displayed alongside flags of many nations and thematic college banners hung high around the perimeter of the store, all of which were popular with the students of the nearby university. The flag brought immediate and deep offense that I neither intended nor immediately understood, an offense borne out of my blindness, ignorance, and privilege as a young man. Pointing to that symbol of racism in our country, she directly confronted me (or in the words of the TRC, told the story), portrayed how deeply the offense impacted her and why (named the hurt), and invited a response from me (sharing our humanity). As I stood filled with guilt at the cash wrap, she challenged me—forcefully so—and when she recognized my utter lack of enlightenment regarding symbols of racism and the Jim Crow South, she invited me into dialogue (attempting to renew and not release the relationship). What grew from her challenge was an acceptance of an invitation to worship in her congregation and an active engagement in self-education on issues of racism, racial justice, and systemic issues rather than relying on people of color to educate me. Rev. Jane challenged me to recognize the history of our country—steeped, as was Tutu's, in racism—and to see the people who have experienced its consequential impact.

The lesson she taught me, like the childish theft at G. C. Murphy's, marked my life and has stayed with me ever since. It was the soil out of which a commitment grew to understand more deeply the history and impact of racism and racial injustice, and a commitment followed, as a bookseller and later as a publisher, to help authors speak powerfully into those issues as well.

Rev. Jane's extended mercy to me that day and in the years that followed, as she once again returned to a store whose product brought such understandable offense, changed me and set me on a path of understanding—if only, thus far, partially— my biases, blind spots, and racism, and that has made a lasting impact on the work I have done in the intervening years.

~

The late ethicist and writer Lewis B. Smedes once remarked that forgiveness "usually takes a cast of two" and that "solitaire forgiving, some people say, makes no more sense than solo tennis."

Smedes disagreed about the solitaire forgiving. I do, as well. In addition to longing for and receiving the forgiveness of God, and the ability to receive and extend forgiveness with others, there is a fourth and distinct longing resident within our souls that I, like most of us, have recognized a need for: forgiving ourselves.

As we navigate the long and winding road that makes up each of our lives, even the most undivided, consistent Christ followers among us stumble: we slip, we fall. The particulars of my own stories that prompted the need of forgiving myself—stories within my family, my workplace; stories with friends I hurt or aid I could have and should have given but failed to do so—are etched in my memory, not for detailing here. What is important to note is the recognition, the awareness of those places of shame within ourselves in need of healing, the need to attend to them and release them to a God who loves us and forgives us.

"We feel a need to forgive ourselves because the part of us that gets blamed feels split off from the part that does the blaming," Smedes writes. "One self feels despised and rejected by the other. We are exiled from our own selves, which is no way to live. This is why we need to forgive ourselves and why it makes sense to do it: We are ripped apart inside, and forgiving ourselves is the only way we heal the split."

What self-forgiveness requires is self-awareness, a brutal honesty with ourselves, an ability to look in the mirror and articulate what we have done. It also relies on the processing (often if not always in community or with a professional counselor) of guilt and shame, and a consideration of steps we may need to take with others we may have harmed. And we can use the telling of our own stories in service to our families, friends, and others.

"We all want to live in peace and harmony. But living in peace with others requires having peace and harmony within ourselves," Desmond Tutu and Mpho Tutu write. "We can transform our guilt and our shame by using our past to be of benefit to others. When we place ourselves and our stories in the service of others, we can more easily forgive ourselves for our failings."

The memories I carry with me of the unwise youthful indiscretion at the G. C. Murphy five-and-dime store, of Rev. Jane's confrontational remarks, gracious extension of forgiveness, and intention of healing, and of the plentiful examples of actions (or inactions) for which I needed to grant forgiveness to myself are but a series of stitches in a tapestry of a lifetime of actions (or inactions) that led to an understanding of my need for forgiveness; that led to a recognition that forgiveness and release come through listening, learning, confession, repentance, and where needed, restitution. They come through a loving God (and loving people) who extend grace and understanding. They come through forgiving ourselves and being released from shame.

Long gone now are the G. C. Murphy's chain of stores. Like many businesses, it was sold out to an impersonal conglomerate, and by 1985 all that was left was its foundation to care financially for former employees who had fallen on hard times. But I'm confident that if we went to the backyard of my old London home, I could show you the place where, if we put a shovel in the dirt, we would find a cultural and spiritual artifact, still intact. My very own time capsule of a day that triggered the longing for forgiveness.

The Longing for Forgiveness
A Playlist

"You Don't Mess Around with Jim," Jim Croce, from the recording *Photographs and Memories* (1974)

"Love at the Five and Dime," Nanci Griffith with Darius Rucker, from the recording *The Dust Bowl Symphony* (1999)

"O Happy Day," the Edwin Hawkins Singers, from the recording *Let Us Go into the House of the Lord* (1968)

"The Heart of the Matter," Don Henley, from the recording *The End of Innocence* (1989)

"Forgiveness," Patty Griffin, from the recording *Living with Ghosts* (1996)

"Forgiving Eyes," Michael Card, from the recording *Scandalon* (1985)

CHAPTER 5

The Longing for Spiritual Transformation

The longing of every heart, and of my heart, is so intense. We want the tears to be gone, the aches to be over. While it is still mysterious to me, through a glass darkly as it is, I think I understand a bit more of the relationship between a whole heart and a broken heart—and I sigh, torn as I am between what I am and what I want to be.

Steven Garber, *The Seamless Life*

To me the jack pine is a most intriguing tree, its life is something like a miracle. Something like resurrection.

Fire is its principal means of survival, its primary pathway to transformation and to life.

Throughout much of Canada jack pine ranges can be found, where its northern boundary extends from the Northwest Territories eastward to Nova Scotia. In the United States, jack pine stands are scattered through Maine, New Hampshire, northern New York, Michigan, northwest Indiana, northeast Illinois, Wisconsin, and Minnesota.

The size of jack pines varies from small, bushy-like trees to more substantial, straight-trunked growth of eighty to one hundred feet. Notably, the jack pine forest is home to the Kirtland's warbler, a bird listed on the US Fish and Wildlife Service's endangered species list until 2019 and remaining on a watch list to this day. The Kirtland's warbler requires young, dense stands of eighty acres or more of jack pine for its unique nesting practices.

All of those things and more make the jack pine forests of North America an interesting study for ornithologists, weekend birders, or students of natural resources and forestry. And while I appreciate and admire birds and forests, I'm none of those things, but the jack pine has somehow captivated my attention. Most alluring for me is the jack pine's relationship to fire and the transformation that comes due to heat emerging at *just* the right frequency, in the right level of intensity, and for the proper length of time, literally creating and sustaining life through what, on the surface, looks like destruction.

For the seeker of spiritual transformation, jack pines have something to offer us as well.

"The seed of the jack pine will not be given up by the cone unless the cone itself is subjected to sustained and concentrated heat," wrote civil rights leader and long-time Howard University chaplain Howard Thurman in his *Meditations of the Heart*, a book published in 1953 just two years before the Montgomery bus boycott would catalyze the long-needed transformation of systems of justice and opportunity for people of color in the United States (still profoundly incomplete nearly three-quarters of a century later).

The forest fire sweeps all before it and there remain but the charred reminders of a former growth and a former beauty. It is then in the midst of the ashes that the secret of the cone is exposed. The tender seed finds the stirring of life deep within itself—and what is deepest in the seed reaches out to what is deepest in life—the result? A tender shoot, gentle roots, until, at last, there stands straight against the sky the majestic glory of the jack pine.

In his meditation on the jack pine, Thurman wisely goes on to suggest that, like the jack pine forest, there are things "deep within the human spirit that are firmly embedded, dormant, latent and inactive," remaining that way until our lives are touched by fire.

～

Over a decade ago my life—dormant, latent, both holding and waiting for new growth—was touched deeply by metaphorical fire. At the time I experienced a profound sense of loneliness: separated from people I loved and uprooted from the rhythms around family, church, and work that had given my life structure and a sense of safety and well-being. Everything felt like it was melting from the heat.

In the fire's wake, I felt a hollowing out of faith, joy, contentment, peace, and certainty that I had long known—or, at least, *thought* I had. Now I felt newly adrift in ways I'd not experienced since the days of my journeys alone as an adolescent down to the railroad trestle that spanned Sugar Creek in London, Indiana.

Six months after the metaphorical fire was at its apex, on a Sunday in the early days of worship at our then new liturgical church, I encountered the hymn "Good Soil," composed by Handt Hanson, the long-time worship arts director (now retired) at Prince of Peace Lutheran Church in Burnsville, Minnesota. At the time Lutheran hymnody was new to me, but the lyric and the melody of Hanson's brief yet evocative hymn captivated me and pulled at my heart in an unusual way. For weeks I could not get its sounds and its plea out of my mind.

"Lord, let my heart be good soil open to the seed of your word," Hanson wrote, and we as a small congregation sang together. "Lord, let my heart be good soil, where love can grow, and peace is understood."

I recall saying to our director of music ministry that day, "I hope we will continue to sing 'Good Soil' in worship! Such a lovely, timely message. It said what I needed to hear today."

Truer might have been, it's what I need to hear every day! Or it's what I'd been longing to hear for months.

By my recollection, since that day more than ten seasons of Ordinary Time ago, we've not sung Hanson's hymn again. And the worship director who had chosen it for that day of fire has now retired. But the words and their appeal to God for the transformation that I needed at that time—and, I believe, we all long for, in varying ways and degrees—have stayed with me.

> Lord, let my heart be good soil,
> open to the seed of your Word.
> Lord, let my heart be good soil,
> where love can grow and peace is understood.
> When my heart is hard,
> break the stone away.
> When my heart is cold,
> warm it with the day.
> When my heart is lost,
> lead me on your way.
> Lord, let my heart,
> Lord, let my heart,
> Lord, let my heart be good soil.

Hanson's words open the heart to the truth of the spiritual transformation process, as he recognizes the reality that it is God's work, through God's Spirit, that warms our cold hearts, that turns us around when we've lost our way; that the soil of our hearts where the seeds of God's word are planted can ultimately grow, in the memorable words of Mother Teresa of Kolkata, into "something beautiful for God."

In some mysterious way, it is often (though decidedly not only) through seasons of fire, heat, or what looks like desolation that new growth arises for us, just as with the jack pine forest. Hanson's words capture the importance of remaining open throughout our lives to the seeds of Scripture and Christ's presence being planted in our hearts and minds through our reading, our listening, our speaking; through times of solitude and times of community; through cycles of joy and wonder, pain and loss. They capture the reality that all of our lives are marked at one time or another by a season of dormancy and cold, in need of the thawing warmth of the Spirit's work in and through us. Sometimes with the fierceness opening the fire cone, sometimes gently like the tulips buried under blankets of snow, life and fresh growth, color, and vibrancy will emerge in the spring.

The great poet T. S. Eliot suggested that poetry makes us "a little more aware of the deeper, unnamed feelings which form the substratum of our being, to which we rarely penetrate; for our lives are mostly a constant evasion of ourselves." Music plays that role for me, driving me either through melody, lyric, or both to a deeper place where I am in touch with deeper, unarticulated feelings, experiences, longings.

～

In the late 1970s Richard J. Foster published a book titled *Celebration of Discipline*, his message to readers about finding the door to liberation through a mixture of inward, outward, and corporate disciplines including solitude, fasting, simplicity, confession, celebration, and other practices. It was at least mildly controversial in the conservative religious circles I was a part of, especially the idea of "Christian meditation," which was the chapter that opened his first section on what he called "inward disciplines." (I'm confident it would *not* have been controversial among Catholic and less conservative Protestant Christians of the day, but I rarely rubbed shoulders with them at the time.)

That book may well have been the first encounter I had with spiritual formation language. And in the years since, it became an important doorway for my spiritual journey, particularly for my understanding of the process of spiritual transformation, which had not been a part of my heritage. Up until that time, I had lived and read in a mostly cerebral space—looking for answers to real or imagined questions that I could file away and pull out in a moment's notice when someone was trying to shoot a hole in my arguments for the existence of God, the reliability of texts, or the uniqueness of Christ. Reading *Celebration of Discipline* felt like drinking a cup of cold water on an unseasonably hot day. It was a new message in many ways, but it spoke to a yearning I'd carried with me to cease being the "Shell Answer Man" and just *be*.

Among the words I read were these: "When we despair of gaining inner transformation through human powers of will and determination, we are open to a wonderful new realization: inner righteousness is a gift from God to be graciously received," Foster wrote. "The needed change within us is God's work, not ours. The demand is for an inside job, and only God can work from the inside. We cannot attain or earn this righteousness of the kingdom of God; it is a grace that is given."

I was not raised in the church, nor did I have exposure to any religious instruction for most of my upbringing. When

I did encounter Christian teaching in my late teens, the emphasis was decidedly on a *moment* of conversion—praying a prayer, inviting God into my heart, and making a change, a turning. I heard phrases like "So if anyone is in Christ, there is a new creation: everything old has passed away; see, everything has become new!" (2 Corinthians 5:17). But that was not my experience. All was *not* new. The old had *not* all passed away, though I most assuredly wanted it to.

"Is it just me who is not entirely new?" I wondered.

As a young adult in my twenties, I was prematurely (and, in hindsight, unwisely) invited into church leadership as an elder of a mid-sized congregation. In short order I was teaching others about Christian discipleship, though I was a stranger to any notion of genuine spiritual transformation and always sensed I was just one banana peel away from losing my balance in the Christian life. In those years as a follower of Christ, I'd been steeped in discipleship as an intellectual exercise in gaining more and more knowledge. Too often, I was focused on information *about* God and the Christian life rather than actually inviting the *experience* of God in my life. And with the apostle Paul in his message to the Roman church, I often found myself asking, "Why do I not do the good I want to do, and do the things I do not want to do?"

In the years that followed, through the reading of Foster's seminal work and others that soon echoed the wisdom of spiritual discipleship, I embraced the reality that "inner righteousness is a gift from God to be graciously received." And I came to see spiritual transformation as a collaborative process with God, not a single moment in time. As a process of being conformed to the image of Christ and living not merely for the sake of myself but for the sake of others. As not merely a set of behaviors whereby I carefully cultivate an image of doing all the "right things" others expected of me. This collaborative process, I also came to see, was enabled by the Holy Spirit, the third portion of the doctrine of the Trinity that was not often talked about in the Christian environments of which I was a part.

Like many other aspects of the Christian life, I came to see spiritual transformation as another mystery.

Writer and retreat leader Ruth Haley Barton is known for focusing her teaching squarely on the path of spiritual transformation in the lives of individuals and organizational leaders. She has suggested that this understanding of mystery is one of the cornerstone truths of spiritual transformation. She teaches that while we can (and should) be open to it, we are wise to realize that we do not accomplish transformation for ourselves.

The rugged individualist in my soul didn't like that answer, but I recognized in her words the sense of rightness.

"The journey of transformation begins with the desire to look at and own the truth about myself. It continues as I face the *larger* truth that I'm unable to permanently change myself without the power of God," Stephen Smith writes in his book *The Transformation of a Man's Heart*. "If I could have, I would have. Nothing short of this sincere desire for change will launch us on the path toward transformation." Smith, who for many years operated a retreat center in the mountains of Colorado called the Potter's Inn, where I stayed on two occasions, goes on to say,

Once we've committed to the journey toward authentic transformation as opposed to the pseudo-transformation tips and techniques or an instant cure-all, our imaginations can help us understand the transformation process. When we envision our hearts as instruments of clay that the Potter shapes and reshapes with strong and loving hands, we relax more. We accept unpredictable circumstances and crises as catalysts for change and transformation. We envision the clay spinning on the wheel and note the different shapes and forms it takes over time.

The jack pine–like fire I experienced more than a decade ago was composed of both personal and professional elements, each affecting the other. Both drove me to more deeply consider what I believed, what I was prepared to let go of, and what was truly essential to my Christian journey. The fire also prompted me to articulate to myself and those closest to me what I needed and how they could help.

∿

Within the longing for transformation and through the process of identifying and probing the other longings of my heart in these pages, I have grown to understand the ways in which God has met me within each longing. I have come to see how our hearts can be formed by liturgies, practices, and imitations oriented to the kingdom of God, and empowered by the Holy Spirit.

The mystery of Christian spiritual transformation is not a collection of knowledge, not a program but rather a collaborative work between each individual and God, and that shift in my understanding has been a critical one for me.

I've offered below a list of several practices that have been transformative for me, knowing (as I do) that they will change—some new added, some older practices dropped—over the remainder of my life. Your pathways may be very different, but if you are looking for a place to start, consider the invitation of one or more of these practices:

- *Consistent reading of the Psalms,* which blend anguish, pleas for change, cries of God's seeming absence, and yet assurances of God's ultimate and present care. There are virtually no human emotions I can name that are not contained in the 150 works of prose and poetry we know as the Psalms. The *Devotional Psalter (ESV)* or the book *In the Lord I Take Refuge* both pair up the Psalms with poignant devotional reflections by pastor and author Dane Ortlund and have been cornerstone resources for me in recent times.

- *Conversation with a spiritual director,* who listens with care and with wisdom reflects words for consideration and asks questions about what God may be saying to me in a given situation. This can be a vulnerable relationship, but once established with a trusted person, it can also be life giving.

- Regular, end-of-day practice of the examen, taking time to reflect even if for ten minutes on the moments of desolation and consolation experienced in the day that just ended. (See chapter on freedom from fear and anxiety for more.)

- Allocating time for a time of retreat, either alone or with others in community, even if it feels (as it has to me, a "responsible" person) as being "irresponsible" or "wasting time with God." You and I are both worth investing time in. A solo retreat, in particular, is what I've found to be a pathway for God to speak into my life in powerful ways.

- Reading collections of prayers and devotional books handed down through the ages, books that distill the wisdom and the universal cries for faith, hope, and love. Among the books that have been most cherished in my own journey are the following:
  - *A Diary of Private Prayer* by John Baillie (1886–1960)
  - *The Temple* by W. E. Orchard (1877–1955)
  - *Meditations of the Heart* by Howard Thurman (1899–1981)
  - *Disciplines of the Inner Life* by Bob Benson and Michael W. Benson
  - *A Guide to Prayer for All God's People* by Rueben P. Job and Norman Shawchuck
  - *Devotional Classics, A Renovaré Resource for Spiritual Renewal*, edited by Richard J. Foster and James Bryan Smith, which introduces

and excerpts the writings of devotional masters including Thomas Merton, Francis de Sales, Julian of Norwich, Frank Laubach, John Baillie, Elizabeth O'Connor, C. S. Lewis, and many others.

— *The Book of Common Prayer*, used for centuries by the Anglican Communion of churches worldwide

— *Be Thou My Vision*, a liturgy for daily worship (including creeds and catechisms), edited and compiled by Jonathan Gibson

- Praying the Divine Hours, particularly as gathered up by the late Phyllis Tickle in her multivolume works of the same title in the Benedictine tradition of fixed-hour praying—morning, midday, and evening through all of the seasons.

- The practice of *Lectio Divina*, or the slow and repeated reading of a single set of Scripture passages, is another discipline that has been key for me, more recently enabled by a podcast called *Daily Lectio Divina*, hosted by author Sharon Garlough Brown and Abiding Way Ministries.

- Finally, the practice of journaling as a spiritual discipline has been an important avenue of spiritual transformation and a way God has consistently met me in this longing of the heart. It is often in my journal that I can seek and metaphorically speak to Christ and hear Christ's invitations to continued spiritual transformation.

As an end-of-the-era baby boomer, I grew up with quick television dinners, instant coffee, microwave ovens, and other means of delivering just what was needed or desired quickly, instantaneously. But Christian spiritual transformation is not like that. It takes time, receptivity, and trust in the God who has given us the tools we need for change. Few of us have Damascus road experiences as did the apostle Paul, and perhaps that's as it should be. Katie Haseltine, an author and instructor on the Ignatian examen, writes that "transformation is less disorienting, less scary when you experience it as gradual and subtle. You might not see the monumental shift taking place—and you might try to stop it if you did—but you can notice the incremental movements toward greater faith, hope, and love."

Each of the above practices has prompted that gradual, subtle, and yet genuine and life-giving transformation of which Haseltine writes.

Among the questions I ask for journaling are these: What will your practices be? What has brought life-giving change thus far? What new paths might you take? Whatever they are, you will be in good company with others down through the centuries who have walked before you, before us all.

"Down through Christian history various spiritual principles, rules, disciplines and practices have aided the believer in the quest for a deeper knowledge of God," Bob Benson and Michael W. Benson write in one of my favorite prayer books.

There were liturgies, lectionaries, prayer books and guides for the hours and days of one's spiritual journey. One of the common threads of all of these tools of spirituality was the recognition of the need for constancy in the establishment and deepening of a person's spiritual relationship with God. And underlying the writings of all those whose works have stood the test of time is the theme of faithfulness and regularity in spiritual practice.

The intense fire of a decade ago and the smaller ones that come as a natural part of all of our lives prompted me to deepen and commit to the regular practice of spiritual disciplines, even on days when I felt like doing anything but that.

~

In Illinois where I live, also known as "the Prairie State," we are just at the southern edge of the jack pine's range. Oak, hickory, maple, birch, and walnut trees are much more common sights in this area than jack pine, and I'm more likely to see a prescribed burn of a planted prairie here than any fire among the jack pines. But the principle of the jack pine carries over to the tallgrass prairie. The heat at just the right time, in just the right intensity, managed with care in late winter or early spring, triggers new life on our native landscape.

Just as it does in our lives. The heat provides nourishment to the soil, and the good soil is fertile ground for new growth, new life, for transformation.

The Longing for Spiritual Transformation
A Playlist

"Transformation," Van Morrison, from the recording *Roll with the Punches* (2017)

"Good Soil," composed by Handt Hanson, from *ELW Hymnal*, #512 (1985)

"I Feel a Change Comin' On," Bob Dylan, from the recording *Together through Life* (2009)

"New Every Morning," Rory Noland, from the recording *The Lord Is in Our Midst* (2013)

"Hallelujah," Michael McDonald, from the recording *Soul Speak* (2008)

"The Circle Game," Joni Mitchell, from the recording *Ladies of the Canyon* (1970)

CHAPTER 6

The Longing for Peace

Long ago, a wise spiritual director said to me, "Ruth, you are like a jar of river water all shaken up. What you need is to sit still long enough that the sediment can settle, and the water can become clear."

Ruth Haley Barton, "Make a Joyful Silence"

The 1960s was a time of both turbulence and idealism, with the ravages of Vietnam that appeared in living rooms nightly on the *CBS Evening News* with Walter Cronkite juxtaposed alongside the pop culture foretelling of an Age of Aquarius where peace would guide the planets and the sun would always be shining. It was a time when the riots in Watts, Detroit, and Newark lived alongside Woodstock's "three days of peace and music" on Max Yasgur's dairy farm in Bethel, New York and the "summer of soul" at the 1969 Black Cultural Festival in Harlem.

President John F. Kennedy's so-called moon shot declaration in 1962 was an idealistic part of a decade in which his vision and NASA's lunar landing bracketed the assassinations of civil rights leaders Martin Luther King and Malcolm X, killings that reflected and triggered yet more turbulence.

It was a time, not unlike our own, of great upheaval, and a time in which a longing for peace in hearts and homes and distant lands was palpable.

As the decade gave way to the 1970s, an unlikely anthem of peace and utopian ideals won a Grammy Award for best spoken recording in 1971. The song was titled "Desiderata," performed by a former television talk show host named Les Crane and released on Warner Brothers Records, the major label that was home to leading artists of the day such as Van Morrison; Peter, Paul, and Mary; and James Taylor. The song peaked at number 8 and spent twelve weeks on Billboard's Hot 100 list of songs that year. Based on a poem published in 1927 by an attorney-turned-writer from Terre Haute, Indiana, named Max Ehrmann, "Desiderata" became known as a poem of peace for generations, and was symbolic of the idealism still resident at the dawn of the new decade, as I was coming of age.

I adorned the wall of my bedroom with a parchment-like copy of "Desiderata" and regularly spun the recording of it on my record player, soaking up its ideals, which stood in stark contrast to the way I experienced much of the world around me and the news I consumed. Through the stereo speakers I would hear Crane's baritone voice rendering Ehrmann's words exhorting us to move placidly amid the noise of the world and to remember the peace one finds in silence; words about being—as far as is humanly possible—on good terms and at peace with others, at peace in our own souls, and at peace with God, whatever we conceived God to be.

It was a compelling vision.

As a person devoid of any connection at that time to a sacred text such as the Bible, the Koran, the Torah, or others tied to mysterious Eastern religions, I was captivated by Ehrmann's words and for a season it became something of a sacred work or guiding philosophy, especially the poet's vision for peace. One of the first gifts the person who would later become my wife gave me after we met in college was a copy of one of Ehrmann's collections of poetry titled *The Desiderata of Happiness*, an anthology of philosophical and religious works, which I have to this day.

Decades have passed and that longing for peace remains within my own soul, interpersonally, and for our planet. But time has demonstrated that the fulfillment of the longing is much more complicated than the sloganeering of popular songs, "give peace a chance" bumper stickers, music festivals, or a spoken word version of an idealistic poem.

But it is possible, even amid personal or societal upheaval.

One thing that Max Ehrmann most definitely got right and that has remained with me: there is wisdom and peace in the practice of silence. And it's one of the ways in which God has met me in the midst of this longing for peace, even to the hum of a peculiar kind of noise.

~

Sanctuary.

The definitions are multifaceted: A safe place. A shrine. A setting for worship. To a refugee or a person fleeing violence or oppression, the word *sanctuary* captures a sense of hoped-for safety and provision. To a birder, it's a special set-aside area in which a long-sought-after species just might be seen, even if at a distance.

To a person in a religious community or church, the word conjures up images of stained glass, icons, people in robes and vestments, sacred texts and hymn books in the backs of uncomfortable wooden seats.

But the seat of a John Deere lawn tractor? Can *that* be a sanctuary?

A whitewashed, nondescript one-car garage sits off to the side of the property whose sign welcomes people to the local Lutheran church I now call home. The garage is some three hundred yards from the gathering place called "sanctuary," with its stained glass on three sides, and adornments draped over lectern, eucharistic table, and baptismal font, from which the word and the sacraments are practiced weekly.

The garage houses no car and has no adornments. Very few people ever visit it. But it held the keys to my midlife sanctuary and brought a sense of peace I was longing for in an important season of my life.

Inside, a John Deere riding lawn mower, with its trademark yellow and green color scheme, sat waiting for a small group of volunteers to arrive—one per week—and tackle the weekly mowing that, from April to October, keeps the church's expansive grounds neat, tidy, orderly, and well presented—a portrait, one could argue, of Lutheran theology itself. While the church's custodian recovered from a health issue, we were asked to fill in.

That January after a season of fallow engagement with a church that we had long called home, my wife asked one Sunday, "What about visiting Faith Lutheran?" I'd never considered attending a Lutheran church. My primary connection to that ecclesial tradition was from reading the books of long-time Lutheran pastor Walter Wangerin Jr. or the classic biography of Martin Luther, *Here I Stand*, written by Roland Bainton.

But I was a bit desperate for community, for a place to call home, for a place of worship more centered on the Eucharist and more accepting of mystery. My soul was parched, thirsty, in need of a cup of cold spiritual water. I harbored a longing for quiet, for peace. In the whirlwind of Western existence with its emphasis on speed, productivity, and technology, I am convinced that we all long for a measure of slowness and peace, even if we live most of our lives without acknowledging it.

"Sure. Why not? I'll go check the service times," I said.

Less than an hour later, we arrived in the sanctuary and attended our first of what has now become more than a decade of Sundays.

As the so-called polar vortex of that winter began to give way to spring and the church calendar moved from Epiphany to Lent, the church's weekly service bulletin included a two-sentence call for volunteers to help with the season's mowing, and my eyes brightened. I immediately sent a message to the coordinator to say I'd be happy to care for the grounds. In more than thirty years of attending churches in Indiana, Tennessee, and Illinois, I was always quick to offer to teach or respond to calls to leadership—visible roles that are often given places of honor and respect; roles that are attached, rightly or not, to a sense of importance, power, prestige.

But mowing a church's property? I'd never been asked, never offered, never done it. But in that year, it seemed just what my soul was in need of. Anonymity. Physicality. Solitude.

With eight or nine people on the mowing crew, each of us had but a few weeks for which we were responsible, and each of the weeks on my calendar were marked in brightly colored, ALL CAPS lettering:

MOWING WEEK. FAITH CHURCH.

I looked forward to each week with expectation, knowing what those hours would bring.

In his book *Walking the Labyrinth*, the writer Travis Scholl says,

On the surface of it, [a labyrinth] is a place for silence and for speaking into silence, for speaking to One unseen. But beneath the surface, walking the labyrinth is a profound discipline in listening, in active silence, in finding movement and rhythm in the stillnesses underneath and in between every day's noise. Walking the labyrinth is an exercise in finding the voice speaking in whispers underneath the whirlwind of sound.

I have walked labyrinths in New Harmony, Indiana, the grounds of arboretums and botanical gardens in North America and the United Kingdom, and on the Dingle Coast of Ireland, and wholeheartedly concur with Scholl about listening for the whispers underneath the whirlwinds of our lives. The "spiritual discipline" of mowing the grounds of the church became for me a type of labyrinth and an avenue to peace. Each of those weeks marked in bright colors and ALL CAPS on my calendar brought three or more hours of sanctuary. They became a time and a place of rest, provision, discovery, peace. A paradoxical place of solitude and silence, amid the hum of a twenty-two-horsepower engine.

In the spring, summer, and fall of that first year of life among the Lutherans, I found a place of solace, prayer, mindfulness, appropriate anonymity, and service that brought life and rekindled a sense of joy and hopefulness that had largely been missing from my experiences associated with church over the prior decade. It became a sanctuary and a path of peace, alongside new vistas in Lutheran hymnody, the reading of Psalms devotionally, and fresh encounters in the natural world.

～

Like the appreciation of classic and modern art, music is an admittedly subjective thing. What sounds like noise to one person is a thing of beauty to another. What feels old fashioned to someone is deeply relevant to another. But in some mysterious way, encountering Lutheran hymnody over the past decade has been a wellspring of peace for my own journey.

Not only did I there meet—transformative moment—the Handt Hanson hymn "Good Soil," but also (and more frequently encountered) the song "Kyrie, Setting 8." The words *kyrie eleison* are a formulation in Greek for our English phrase "Lord, have mercy," and in the liturgical church tradition are "used as a preliminary petition before a formal prayer and as a congregational response in the liturgies of many Christian churches." *Kyrie* is the title given to Christ, in portions of Scripture such as in Philippians 2:11.

In advance of taking the Eucharist each week, it's customary for us to sing a *Kyrie Eleison* with words that form a holistic view of the peace and nourishment that is possible in our lives, our communities, and our world as we seek to do justice, to love kindness, and to walk humbly with our God (Micah 6:8).

Kyrie, Setting 8

For peace in the world, for the health of the church,
for the unity of all, For this holy house,
for all who worship and praise
Let us pray to the Lord

That we may live out your impassioned response to
    the hungry and the poor
That we may live out truth and justice and grace
Let us pray to the Lord

For peace in our hearts, for peace in our homes, for
    friends, and family
For life and for love, for our work and our play
Let us pray to the Lord

For your Spirit to guide, that you center our lives in
  the water and the Word
That you nourish our souls with your body and
  blood
Let us pray to the Lord

Kyrie eleison, on our world and on our way
Kyrie eleison, every day.

As we sing these words I am reminded of the scope of Christ's work, care, and granting of peace. As we sing, I am reminded of the connection between our worship and our work in the world, seeking justice, caring for the poor. As we sing, I am reminded again and anew of the work of Christ on the cross and the pathway that was forged for us to have peace with God, to be reconciled with God. And I am reminded that our work in the world is not done alone. *God is with us. Immanuel. A risen Savior.*

Music is a primary pathway of peace, something I know isn't true for everyone. Important is attentiveness to that which nurtures peace in our hearts and minds, not necessarily the specific avenue. Becoming aware of what stirs us up and what calms us down; what triggers tension and anxiety and what breathes life and rest and peace into our souls is important, even amid the good work we want (and must) do in the world.

~

The natural world is another sacred pathway to peace, and I discovered that pathway near streams and on prairies.

Belmont Prairie, situated between a housing development and an interstate freeway, is an unlikely place for some of the highest-quality remnant tallgrass prairie plants in all of northern Illinois, a state whose motto has since at least 1842 been "the Prairie State," though little of its original landscape remains.

A brief written history of the Belmont Prairie suggests that a man by the name of John Graves in 1842 purchased two sections of prairie land from the US government. A portion of his land was later developed into a golf course, while the rest was left undeveloped.

"Then, in April of 1970, Alfred and Margaret Dupree presented a photograph of a rare prairie wildflower to an expert at the Morton Arboretum, as they were interested if it represented possible remnants of a native prairie. Upon inspection, it was found that the field had numerous native prairie species, and with the help of The Nature Conservancy, the owners were tracked down and the land was purchased. After officially becoming a part of the Park District, it was named an Illinois Nature Preserve in March, 1994," the site's brief history states.

One of the great joys of living in northern Illinois is my frequent hikes with my wife, Cindy, through the area's tallgrass prairies, the original but vanishing landscape of our state. We typically travel together to the prairie and then split up on the trails, where she brings a camera to take photos of the native grasses, insects, and more, and I carry my journal, often finding a spot to rest and reflect on the landscape within, the landscape without.

On a late April hike of Belmont Prairie near the office where I worked at the time, six weeks into a work-from-home order due to the global pandemic that began in 2020, my eyes were lifted from the line of grasses up to the top of a tree. Something was uncharacteristically fluttering in the treetop of this otherwise pastoral setting.

A kite.

Stuck in the top of a burr oak, a kite in the shape of an angry-looking shark was fluttering in the springtime winds, struggling to free itself from bare branches and regain lift, freedom, flow.

The symbolism struck me immediately. The kite became a metaphor for what we as people in our country and around the world had experienced because of the pandemic and its accompanying economic crisis. We, like that kite, were seemingly held in a state of suspension, longing for the natural rhythms, flow, life, and lift to return. We were longing for peace.

Throughout the months since, we have returned to Belmont Prairie with frequency, walking the trails, crossing creeks, watching sandhill cranes migrate overhead and deer graze in the big bluestem grasses below. The silence, the beauty, and the resilience of the prairie through all seasons even as the global pandemic raged on have been beacons of peace, and on many occasion I have taken a pocket edition of the Old Testament book of Psalms with me to read devotionally, finding there the lament, the praise, and the reassurance of peace to reappear.

~

Praying the Psalms, too, in a daily, meditative manner has increasingly become a pathway to peace. In them I encounter a depth of emotion, from lament to thanksgiving, from anguish to joy.

In the *Renovaré Life with God Bible* there's a meaningful introduction to these small passages of lyrics for songs sung long ago:

> The Psalms embrace the wide experience and insight of the community of faith. So we have a great variety: hymns of praise, lament, and thanksgiving; songs recalling God's active presence in Israel's history; songs rooted in prophetic and wisdom teaching; songs of repentance and trust; songs about the king's and God's rule and songs of longing and hope and irrepressible joy.

Throughout the Psalms, I read these songs and am confronted by the holiness and care of a God who is with us, even in the midst of our torments.

Thomas Merton once said, "In the last analysis, it is not so much what we get out of the Psalms that reward us, as what we put into them. If we really make them our prayer, really prefer them to other methods and expedients, in order to let God pray in us His own words, and if we sincerely desire above all to offer Him this particularly pure homage of our Christian faith, then indeed we will enter into the meaning of the Psalms, and they will become our favorite vocal prayers."

And I would add, they will become like landscapes, like the tallgrass prairie—places of peace.

~

We long for peace in profoundly personal ways, in our own lives, in our families, and in our communities. But we must also carry a centuries-old longing for peace throughout the world. We who follow Christ follow the Prince of Peace and understand part of our role in the world is to bring truth, justice, mercy, and humility as we walk the with-God life.

"Changed lives must implement the mission of peace through the changing of society," former US Senator Mark O. Hatfield (1922–2011) wrote. "So we go forth into the world seeing new possibilities, grasping for God's vision" of what God can do. "We have the certain hope that God can impart new life—new life to individuals, to nations, and to all creation. That hope is based in the Risen Christ. All history is consummated in him. He is our Peace."

I'm convinced the lives of people marked by inner peace—carrying the assurance of the leading of the Prince of Peace—are those most able to effect change in the world.

What are the paths to peace? For each of us, we find unique answers. But taking time to consider and experience a variety of pathways—nature, the reading of Scripture, music, writing poetry, praying the Psalms, investing in a solo retreat in solitude and silence, journaling, wilderness moments, or a number of other things call us to find what fills our well, to invest in that path.

~

Although he earned a law degree from Harvard University in Massachusetts, Max Ehrmann, the accomplished poet who wrote his best-known work "Desiderata" in 1927, lived most of his life in the small midwestern city of Terre Haute not far from the banks of the Wabash River, popularized in a famous song written by his friend, Paul Dresser. Ehrmann was known to take long walks along the city's streets, the riverside, and not far from there in Deming Park, the same city park where my maternal family gathered for annual reunions for decades.

Ehrmann's "most cherished hours for writing were in the midnight silence. Afternoons, under the beech trees of Deming Park, he would often sit listening to the silent voice within—that inner voice which Balzac said, 'supports a man of gifts in his moments of despair,'" the poet's widow, Bertha K. Ehrmann, wrote in *Max Ehrmann: A Poet's Life*. "Here in the quiet woods he often found the peace of soul that he brought back to the confused world in his poems. Contemplation of the great forests, green fields, and quiet streams gave him serenity."

Out of that serenity, he penned words that continue to impact lives. I still return to the words "Go placidly amid the noise and haste, and remember what peace there be in silence" and his exhortation to "as far as possible, without surrender, be on good terms with all persons." I appreciate his other admonitions about relationships, tending to our careers, eschewing cynicism, and more. In many ways it was a poem of its time, but its vision for peace is one I return to with more sober discernment than I had as an idealistic teenager.

Today, if you travel to the corner of Wabash Avenue and Seventh Street in Terre Haute, you will discover a bronze sculpture of Ehrmann sitting on a park bench not far from where he wrote many of his best-known poems. Nearby, the words of "Desiderata" are mounted, reminding passersby of the philosophy that animated the idealism of prior generations. The sculpture of the man sitting on the bench, with pen in hand, looks very much at peace, and full of joy.

As the years increase, and our longing for peace grows within us, may we too discover the pathways that bring us to peace and full joy.

The Longing for Peace
A Playlist

"Peace (A Communion Blessing from St. Joseph's Square)," Rich Mullins, from the recording *A Liturgy, a Legacy, and a Ragamuffin Band* (1993)

"Desiderata," Les Crane, from the recording *Desiderata* (1971)

"Kyrie Eleison," Hildegard von Bingen, from the recording *Heavenly Revelations: Hymns, Sequences, Antiphons, Responds*, directed by Jeremy Summerly (1995)

"Morning Has Broken," Cat Stevens, from the recording *Teaser and the Firecat* (1971)

"I've Gotta Find Peace of Mind," Ms. Lauryn Hill, from the recording *MTV Unplugged 2.0* (2002)

"Give Me Love (Give Me Peace on Earth)," George Harrison, from *Living in the Material World* (1973)

PART II

OUR EXTERIOR LONGINGS

We long for a world of goodness and beauty, of
biblical justice, of putting all things right. We
long for a world in which our relationships with
those of the other gender, ethnic people group,
and political party, as well as with the material
world, are governed by kindness and honesty.
Curtis Thompson

CHAPTER 7

The Longing for Community

The more thankfully we daily receive what is given to us, the more assuredly and consistently will community increase and grow from day to day as God pleases.

Dietrich Bonhoeffer, *Life Together*

I t was a bright, unseasonably hot late spring day amid the rolling green hills of Middle Tennessee when the call came through to the office of Scott Roley, a long-time musician, recording artist, pastor, activist, and friend.

It was the call of community.

The person on the other end of the line was Denny Denson, the pastor of First Missionary Baptist Church in Franklin and Scott's spiritual brother in what was known as the Empty Hands Fellowship, a multiethnic assembly that broke bread (or sausage biscuits) at the local McDonald's restaurant on Tennessee Highway 96 every Wednesday morning at 8.

As the call came in, I was sitting on the other side of Scott's desk preparing to talk to him about the next steps for a manuscript that would become his book *God's Neighborhood: A Hopeful Journey in Racial Reconciliation and Community Renewal.* As I listened to his side of the conversation, I realized that the plan for the day—working on marketing strategies, publicity campaigns, and market positioning for the book—was about to be thrown out the window.

Placing the church office phone back on its cradle, Scott got up and said, "Come with me. We have a community need we've got to tend to. We'll get back to this work later."

Taking Scott's lead, I jumped into his mud-soaked Jeep with tackle boxes and fishing poles arcing over the back seat and rode with him to a ramshackle home in a section of suburban Franklin that I didn't know existed. There, we were met by Denny Denson, who explained that he'd received a call that morning from a woman whose grandchildren were having trouble breathing and she didn't know why. She'd said she was fearful they might die.

Stepping inside the house, we said hello to the grandmother and her daughter, holding two young children. The home was sweltering. Flies were swarming around the entryway, and the smell of mold or mildew was overpowering. It took all of one minute to figure out where the issue stemmed from. Denny, Scott, and I followed the smell to the back of the four-room home and started pulling a stove and refrigerator away from the walls, exposing black mold snaking its way, like a deep, ugly bruise, up the length of the drywall—the source of the young children's breathing issues.

Scott and Denny promptly told the grandmother that she needed to get her daughter and grandchildren out of the home. They asked her if the family had somewhere to go, but the woman tearfully shook her head, signaling they had nowhere to turn.

Which is why she had called Denny. She'd heard that First Missionary Baptist Church helped people with few resources.

As I looked on in silence, Scott and Denny told the three-generation family to pack up what they needed, and they would return in about two hours. They let the family know they would mobilize a crew to tend to the mold issue, but they simultaneously would also look for an alternative place for them to live.

Ultimately, these men from Empty Hands Fellowship—one African American, one white, both committed to Christian community—helped the family move to new and safer housing.

"It was just another incident in so many cases where housing, healthcare, and other essentials are unavailable to our community's neediest people," Scott Roley told me years later as we reflected on that incident.

For me, that day prompted introspection, offered instruction, and served as a challenge. It brought me in touch with a longing for community-in-service that was deeper and more radical than I had known up until that time. I returned home asking myself a series of questions:

Would anyone have called me with such a need? What would I have done if they had? Would I have been so preoccupied with my plan for that business day that I might not have considered helping someone in need?

I didn't like the answers I had to my own questions.

"Community cannot take root in a divided life. Long before community assumes external shape and form, it must be present as seed in the undivided self: only as we are in communion with ourselves can we find community with others," Parker Palmer wrote instructively on the barriers we often face. "Community is an outward and visible sign of an inward and invisible grace, the flowing of personal identity and integrity into the world of relationships."

Scott Roley and Denny Denson came from diverse backgrounds—one from privilege, higher education, and access to the halls of power in Washington, DC, where his father had worked in the John F. Kennedy administration; the other came from economic challenges in the shadows of the Civil War South but also incredibly strong family structures and faith as solid as Tennessee flagstone. Even in the differences, God had called them together in community development through the work of John Perkins in Jackson and Mendenhall, Mississippi. It was there that Roley saw community development in action.

"Obviously, God's Word gives us the charge to love God, love our neighbors, and to do so until the whole world knows of God's love," Roley told me. "That is the basis for all of the work that Denny and I and Empty Hands did, and it never got more sophisticated than that. If our community confessed a physical need, we would find a way to meet it—housing, education, medical, healthy food, clean water, legal advice. Every association, every gathering we started was to meet a need brought to us by the people."

Their example reminded me of the words of another member of the Empty Hands Fellowship, a musician named Michael Card:

> And the call is to community
> The impoverished power that sets the soul free
> In humility, to take the vow
> That day after day we must take up the basin and
> the towel.

Card's song "The Basin and the Towel" arose from his study of Scripture as well his work in community alongside Roley, Denson, and others in the Empty Hands Fellowship. The most significant parts of our spiritual growth, he says, take place in the context of community of one kind or another.

"The truths I've learned from Scripture are only actualized in the context of community," Card has told me. "Community offers us all those things isolation robs us of: the encouragement of the brothers and sisters, their insights into our problems, the persistent presence that keeps reminding us we are not alone, their unqualified acceptance that loves us more when we fail."

If he were still here today, Denny Denson would raise his voice with a hearty "amen!" to that, Roley says. As Roley describes it, the call to community for both of them was primarily one of responding to the physical needs of families and individuals, and they took up that basin and towel day after day in their Middle Tennessee community.

For me, who sustained a deep longing for building, nurturing, and maintaining community, to see Roley and Denson sharing their lives in that way, was the first of several gifts pointing me in new directions. It was a profound start. But God's response to my longing for community came in two decidedly different—though no less important—packages.

~

The aftermath of the United States' national election of 2016 sent shock waves through individuals, families, neighborhoods, and the nation as a whole. Divisions and brokenness already present intensified dramatically. Wounds and prejudices and destructive ideologies deeply rooted and deeply felt were laid bare for all the world to see around the country in places like Charlottesville, in detention centers along the Texas-Mexico border, and amid travel bans and refugee suspensions, among a host of other places and issues.

On a winter night as the bleak news stories piled up on top of one other like the layers of snow outside our window, my wife and I contemplated our responses to all that was swirling around us. We shared a desire to bring together a diverse community that would, for an evening on a regular basis, be free of the polarizing tenor of the day. Our mutual desire was to foster community in the midst of those days when it felt like every seam on our country's garment was pulling apart.

"What can *we* do," we wondered, "to cultivate a sense of peace, beauty, and joy in these tense days? What might bring people—even those who see the world (and politics) radically differently—together?"

Our answer came in the form of two things we love, two places God routinely meets us in our respective journeys.

Books. And nature.

Beginning that winter and continuing for several years thereafter, we hosted an ever-expanding group of people in our suburban home every third or fourth month with a simple meal of soup and bread topped off with hot or iced tea (depending on the season), wine, and sparkling water. Normally about forty and up to as many as seventy people came, and after the meal we would take seats scattered like a messy high school band throughout the main level of our home and listen as an author spoke on his or her recently published (or in-process) work. The community heard men and women read poetry, fiction, essays, nonfiction, and hard-to-categorize genres.

As a gathering we covered a mosaic of topics, from the plight of the passenger pigeon to the fall and rise of monarch butterflies. We heard of the exploits of "trickster coyote" and were inspired to care for the tallgrass prairie. We heard a reading about cabin fever and another about the flora and fauna of the Chicago region. We heard about Joy Morton and his founding of the prestigious Morton Arboretum, situated less than two miles from our home. We set up a gallery of a painter's exquisite work and listened as he talked about his creative process, traveling the region's Fox River north to south, painting the water, wildlife, and vegetation in winter, spring, summer, and fall. With the gallery as a backdrop, we listened as he read from a journal he had written to accompany the artwork.

In all seasons people came to listen. Community was built. Beauty was seen. There was unity in diversity, and it was good.

Cindy and I talked about how we, with our skills and interests, might build community. We knew it wouldn't quite be a Roley and Denson approach, but it would invite gathering, beauty, and shared humanity.

"Community is an ongoing entering into friendship, for the mystery of community is that of friends, and the giving of our lives for our friends," Bishop Seraphim Sigrist writes in *A Life Together*, a collection of essays exploring what Christians in the West can learn from the Eastern church. "This friendship is the ongoing gift of the ever deeper realization of the law of sharing and exchange, living Jesus' command to 'bear one another's burdens.'"

What we affectionately called our "books and nature community" did bear one another's burdens amid the tension of those days, though I'm not sure we saw it as emerging out of Jesus's command to do so. We simply were drawn by beauty, goodness, and a sense of the common good.

"We liked getting together with people who wanted to listen attentively to each other and to the guest speaker. The evenings were a time set aside to open one's mind without agenda or pretense and connect with people in a way that was different than our usual transactional ways of dealing with one another," remarked one person who regularly attended these gatherings. "It was a community learning experience without performance pressure where each person could absorb what was new to them personally and sense what was new to others. It was a chance to relax and appreciate each other in an accepting atmosphere. The dinners provided an opportunity for community sharing of both new perspectives and our common affinities for each other and our interests. They were calming events in a stress-filled world."

Another regular attendee and occasional guest speaker at the books and nature gathering added a slightly different vantage point.

"We were gathered around a general interest in nature, writing, and reading. There was nothing overtly religious about this, but from my perspective everyone seemed to be engaged in what I would call 'God's work.' The feeling of urgency about our stewardship of the earth comes, in part, from awareness of the long history of human carelessness for creation," he told me. "But it also comes from a deep, almost unconscious, spiritual awareness that we have an ultimate aim or purpose in this world."

As the global pandemic forced the majority of the world into isolation for an extended period of time, these evenings came to a halt, each person sequestered in their homes. We each felt a significant sense of loss and wondered, "Will we ever be able to gather in community like that again, free of fear?"

But even so, and in the midst of the darkness of those days, new experiences of community arose, and God was present in a deep longing of the heart. Community, I learned, comes in many different shapes and sizes.

∼

In the spring of 2020, as much of the world's commerce, cultural institutions, schools, and governmental offices shut down amid the mysterious and rapidly spreading novel coronavirus, a collective of Chicagoland-based publishers shifted from a pattern of meeting every third month for lunch at a local café to meeting every Tuesday morning via video technology.

Each of the publishers rightly viewed the others as competitors. After all, they bid on the same manuscripts, vied for retention of the same authors, positioned similar books in a crowded marketplace, and talked within their respective companies about market share, growth, profitability, and more. But they also viewed one another as members of a community committed to publishing resources that met needs in the lives of readers around the world. Each viewed the others first as sisters and brothers, and only secondly as competitors. Grief and lament were expressed openly and unreservedly, as were prayers for courage and belief and hope. Practical suggestions for how to navigate the tsunami-like economic waves tearing through the industry were a weekly feature of the meetings.

It was yet another expression of a call to community. And those meetings continued for months thereafter, even when the original impetus for the virtual meetings had passed. It had become yet another way of bearing up one another's burdens.

In an essay on the spiritual discipline of community, Adele Calhoun has suggested that human persons belong together, not apart, reflecting God's "holy community of three." We best express God's nature when we are in community "committed to growing and being transformed into Christlikeness."

In the midst of the darkness that descended in that pandemic spring, the community found among the people whose faces and voices took up residence in tiny boxes on a computer screen was sustaining and healing. We found light in the midst of the shadows that enveloped us.

~

Scott Roley, the friend I was visiting who dropped the business meeting on that unseasonably hot May morning in Tennessee to help people in his community who were in need, tells me that loving our neighbors and being in genuine community with others isn't hard. It's not rocket science. But most people don't respond to the call, he says, because in a certain way it *does* cost you your own life. That's the gift and the cost. As we seek community and tend to the needs arising out of knowing and loving our neighbors, we begin to live as though we were always on call to help because it is God's priority for us.

If I'm honest, I don't always like the idea of being on call for others. It takes me out of my comfort zone and seems countercultural in so many ways. And being in community in even the lesser ways such as opening a home to dozens of other souls for dinner challenges my individualistic tendency, my desire to always put my very best self in front of people as I meet with them, and a propensity for never being in debt to another—to always have my deposits exceed any withdrawals I make from another person.

But being in community with others is worth the cost, worth the challenge, worth the vulnerability.

I think of that woman, her daughter, and two grandchildren in the sweltering-hot home in middle Tennessee, all made in the image of God, each a precious soul. I think of the way Denson and Roley stepped into the need, joyfully and fully, and I know it was but one episode among hundreds that arose and that they responded to throughout the years they broke bread (or sausage biscuits) at the McDonald's on Highway 96.

By now, the two children held at the hips of their mother would be in their twenties. They would not remember the two men who came into that home, pulled the stove away, made arrangements for the mold to be dealt with—they wouldn't remember the others who found them temporary housing, who made it all seem like it wasn't a big deal, it was just what needed to be done.

But I do. I remember it often. And I still hold on to their challenge to live and respond in community as a result. I know a lot of others do too.

The Longing for Community
A Playlist

"What's Going On," Marvin Gaye, from
the recording *What's Going On* (1971)

"You Are Not Alone," Mavis Staples, from
the recording *You Are Not Alone* (2010)

"Brother to Brother," Scott Roley, from
the recording *Brother to Brother* (1986)

"The Basin and the Towel," Michael Card,
from the recording *Poiema* (1994)

"If You're Ready (Come Go With Me)," the Staple
Singers, from the recording *Be What You Are* (1973)

"Get Together," the Youngbloods, from
the recording *The Youngbloods* (1967)

CHAPTER 8

The Longing for Friendship

There's a marked difference between acquaintances and friends. Most people really don't become friends. They become deep and serious acquaintances. But in a friendship you get to know the spirit of another person; and your values coincide.

Maya Angelou

The town of Dwight is nestled in the corn and soybean fields of Illinois, 75 miles southwest of Chicago and 220 miles northeast of St. Louis, Missouri.

It is home to roughly four thousand souls, and its heyday as a railroad town in the late nineteenth and early twentieth centuries has long passed, but the Lincoln service Amtrak train still stops there daily on its journey from Chicago to St. Louis. The downtown streets feature a number of interesting second-hand stores, restaurants, a historic train depot, and the regal Pioneer Gothic Church, built in 1857 and added to the National Register of Historic Places in 1983, with its impressive spire visible at some distance.

The famed, nostalgic Route 66 passed through Dwight beginning in 1921, and the Ambler's Texaco Gas Station, which takes its name from Basil Ambler, the man reported to have run the business from 1938 to 1966, now serves no gasoline. Rather, it serves as Dwight's welcome center and has since 2002 been a part of the US National Park Service's Route 66 Corridor Preservation Program.

Inside Ambler's, elderly gentlemen will proudly show you a framed map of the world mounted on the wall with multicolored push pins stuck in it, indicating the countries from which visitors have traveled. Countries in Europe are filled with a much higher density of push pins than much of the United States, and the docents will wax eloquent about their conversations with people from Denmark, Sweden, Austria, France, Switzerland, and other distant locales—men and women drawn to the old historic road and the tales of adventure, intrigue, and "kicks on route 66," as immortalized in the popular song recorded by the Nat King Cole Trio in 1946. Interpretive signs next to Ambler's begin to tell the story of the iconic route, and others can be found in a nearby rest area to add more texture to the story.

While Dwight holds its place in the history of "kicks" once found on Route 66, for me the small town holds something else: the seedbed of friendship.

Specifically, spiritual friendship.

It's the place I learned lessons about what it meant to enter deeply into a spiritual friendship—to receive it, extend it, nourish it. It was the geographic location in which an *anam cara*, or "soul friend," in the language of the late Irish poet and spirituality writer John O'Donohue, was found, and a deep longing of the heart was met.

"In everyone's life, there is a great need for an *anam cara*, a soul friend. In this love, you are understood as you are without mask or pretension," O'Donohue writes in his book *Anam Cara: A Book of Celtic Wisdom*.

Writer Garry Crites, in an essay on spiritual friendship in *Christian History* magazine, introduces the Middle Irish spelling, *anamchara*, describing how Irish monks brought the tradition to the island of Iona and how they would have understood it. "Soul mate," he says, entirely misses their understanding of the term. And even thinking of a term representing one's closest friend, while closer, still is not complete. "At the core of what makes an *anamchara* is spiritual concern. It is not a term of camaraderie; it is essentially penitential," Crites writes. "The *anamchara* was for Irish Christians the spiritual mentor to whom believers revealed the darkest corners of their hearts—knowing that these beloved guides would support the disciples, confront their sin, and provide remedy."

~

The town of Dwight is midway between the bustling Chicago suburbs and the flat, fertile fields of Bloomington, Illinois. So, its choice as the place where an *anam cara* was discovered was purely utilitarian. At regular intervals, a pastor from the prairie and I would calendar an extended lunch and meet at the Route 66 Diner, or the now-defunct Country Mansion Restaurant, or a hipster barbecue joint just off the town's main street. The food was (and is) incidental, but the time together over a number of years became surprisingly sustaining.

"Soul friends are not content to relegate conversations to small talk, information and emotions," Keith R. Anderson writes in *Friendships That Run Deep*, "but push the curtains back on the windows of honesty and transparency of the soul."

Anderson's depiction of a soul friendship is a succinct portrait of the friendship that developed. A suburban publisher and the pastor from the prairie—it wasn't immediately clear how a friendship even developed. On the surface, we were (and are) *very* different people: A tall, pickup-driving, country music–loving pastor of a large evangelical church. A comparatively short, compact sedan–driving, jazz- and pop music–loving publisher who is a part of a liturgical congregation. But over numerous meals of barbecue briskets and sweet iced tea or scrambled eggs and toast in Dwight, through correspondence and phone calls in between, we discovered a common story in the deep fractures with our respective fathers, holding an underlying theme of disappointment and grief. Together, we explored the similar root reasons and impact not only on us, but on our family systems. God used these shared experiences to bind and bless what became an *anam cara* friendship.

Marked by an attentiveness to what was stirring within our respective souls and a sometimes sense of how God was undeniably present or seemingly absent in a given season of our lives, when we met in Dwight, we talked about words processed in journals as well as unwritten matters of the heart. Trust grew. And we held each other accountable in ways unique in my experience. Probing questions were followed with deep listening.

A spiritual friend, we agreed, is someone who enters our life as a gift from God. They are not intrusive. They are an extra set of ears and eyes into how the grace of God is at work in our life. With that spiritual friend, we are unafraid.

"Ordinary friendships are generally characterized by intimacy, trust and mutual enjoyment of one another," Mindy Caliguire, the founder of Soul Care, a spiritual formation ministry, writes. "Spiritual friends share those qualities, of course, but are also characterized by another element: spiritual friends actively help us pay attention to God."

We are living in a day that is hyperconnected through social media, but lives are often marked by loneliness. There's a longing that we often do not even know how to name for friendship marked by something deeply significant and sustaining to us.

～

A retired social scientist and educator, David W. Smith has spent much of his adult life studying, writing, and speaking about friendship.

On a hot August day, Smith and I talked about the urgency of crafting friendships and the steps we can take to make room for them.

"Friendships are often difficult to form but are essential if we are to experience a well-balanced and enjoyable life," Smith told me. "The greatest indicator of our emotional and spiritual health is how well we're connected to other people."

Smith, the founder of Forming Connections, an organization focused on supporting life-giving friendships, suggested that for friendships to sustain us, it's important to assess the state of our friendships. Asking ourselves a series of questions can be helpful. Questions such as,

- Who would you turn to if your whole world caved in?
- Who would you trust enough to share your intimate thoughts, fears, and frustrations with?
- Who in your life would drop everything to help you during a difficult time?
- Why do some friendships fall apart?
- What's involved in making and keeping satisfying and worthwhile friendships?

In one of his books, Smith alluded to a plaque on his wall that said, "A friend is one who knows you as you are, understands where you've been, accepts who you've become, and still gently invites you to grow."

Friendships are built on principles such as covenant, faithfulness, social involvement, self-disclosure, and candor, Smith says. They include respect, attentive listening, acceptance, empathy, loyalty, and compromise.

~

Spiritual friendships often have the sense of gathering and gift despite ourselves, and they can be formed in an unlikely meeting of hearts. One unlikely friendship that grew between a priest and a minister turned TV personality has served as an instructive portrait regarding how such relationships are developed over time, despite physical distance, and why they are so important to cultivate.

Henri J. M. Nouwen and Fred "Mister" Rogers were both prolific in their own way over more than four decades in public life of a sort, one as a college educator and writer of beloved spiritual wisdom, and the other as a children's television show creator, host, and advocate.

Nouwen, born in Nijkerk, Netherlands, was an author, speaker, priest, and professor at the divinity schools at Harvard and Yale. He left those positions in his later years to serve at L'Arche Daybreak community in Ontario, caring for and living with adults with special physical and developmental needs.

Rogers was born in Latrobe, Pennsylvania, into a well-to-do family. An ordained Presbyterian minister, his "congregation" comprised children reached via television in a make-believe neighborhood, in a show that tackled serious concerns in sensitive, instructive ways. He was an educator on the emotional development of children, a writer, and a speaker.

Both of these men had an enduring impact on my life through their writings, speaking, and their respective examples of attentive care for others, including the most vulnerable among us. I know that has been true of countless others as well.

What was it about both Nouwen and Rogers that has made their impact on lives today so strong—not just during the prime of their careers? Why have documentaries featured these men, and why has a feature film with Tom Hanks, no less, been made on Rogers's life?

As I've considered how they have drawn and mentored others, I realize both Nouwen and Rogers had lives deeply marked by Paul's description of the fruit of the Spirit in his letter to the Galatian church. Among the markers of that fruit are these: gentleness, kindness, and humility. But Nouwen and Rogers not only shared those marks of the Spirit. They were also *anam cara* friends, kindred spirits who spent time together in person on occasion but regularly spoke via telephone. On their respective journeys in a world in which they both seemed oddly and beautifully out of step with the prevailing tenor and tone of their days, their soul-friendship was sustaining and generative.

After Nouwen died, Rogers contributed an essay titled "In the Journey, We Need Friends" to the book *Nouwen Then: Personal Reflections on Henri*. "Henri's death has confirmed for me the enormous power of silence," Rogers wrote in his tribute essay. "Even though most of the world knows Henri best by his words, I've come to recognize his deepest respect for the still, small voice among the quiet of eternity. That's what continues to inspire me."

Christopher de Vinck is a long-term New Jersey educator and the author of more than a dozen collections of spiritual essays, and shared a deep friendship with *both* Rogers and Nouwen. Chris de Vinck's friendship with Nouwen arose through a mutual love of poetry and the fact that they were both writers. His friendship with Fred Rogers developed because, as de Vinck told me, they were both powerfully alike in their spiritual lives and in the way they tended to others.

Fred dearly loved his wife, his two sons and his grandchildren. Fred was emotionally gentle and strong, nonjudgmental, and a man of great faith. He laughed easily, loved a good joke, and prayed often. Fred was an American father to a broad range of children and adults who knew him either through his TV programs or knew him personally.

Henri knew that his loneliness and sense of brokenness was his own to bear, and yet Fred took on Henri's sorrows as he listened with patience and generosity. Their friendship endured in joy because Henri was his complete, open self in Fred's presence and Fred was attentive, nonjudgmental, and filled with empathy and felt blessed that he could add advice and comfort to Henri during his times of great joy and struggle.

As de Vinck spoke about the friends, I understood in a new way the value of *anam cara* friendship—something we continue to long for.

"We have colleagues, neighbors, acquaintances, and we have family members, and all these relationships have boundaries, social cues, acceptable expectations, and walls," de Vinck said to me.

I deeply cared for and admired my colleagues in my education career, but I didn't share with them my regrets or my inner turmoil. My family knows me as husband, father, son, brother, but I do not tell them about my fear of death or my deeply felt omens of sorrow concerning people who have abandoned me. There is one relationship that ties them all together and that is a deeply felt friendship with another that matters, a place where I can be 100 percent myself in all aspects in what it means to be a human being with my flaws, talents, regrets, and joys.

When I met Fred Rogers at the HBO studios over thirty years ago, we became fast friends. For eighteen years there wasn't a week that went by where I didn't receive a card from Fred in the mail, or a letter, or a phone call.

From his friendship with Rogers, Christopher de Vinck learned that deep friendship includes trust, vulnerability, and being in the full presence of the other. "Fred often said that the greatest gift you can give someone is your complete, honest self. Love is a balance between two people, both filling in the missing spiritual gaps of the other with empathy, joy and generosity."

~

For me—and, I suspect, for many of us—the type of friendship Nouwen, Rogers, and de Vinck enjoyed has more often than not been aspirational rather than a reality. *Anam cara* friendship, as I've shared with J. K., the pastor on the prairie, is a unique one, not something I've experienced with many others. Too often some mixture of pretense, caution, utilitarian purposes, or a rugged individualist streak enters in and impedes the type of friendship that leads to a deep knowing and being known and, in turn, to human flourishing. Cultivating such relationships is rare, and requires attention. They seldom fall into our laps.

~

In a remarkable chapter in his bestselling book *Gentle and Lowly*, the author and pastor Dane Ortlund prompts his readers to ponder the question of our relationships, especially our friendship with God, and with others.

There are some people in our lives whose name we know, but they're really on the periphery of our affections. Others are closer to the middle, but perhaps not intimate friends. Continuing to move toward the center, some of us are blessed to have a particularly close friend or two, someone who really knows us and 'gets' us, someone for whom it is simply a mutual delight to be in each other's company. To many of us, God has given a spouse as our closest earthly friend.

Even walking through this brief thought experiment, of course, ignites pockets of mental pain. Some of us are forced to acknowledge that we do not have one true friend, someone we could go to with any problem knowing we would not be turned away. Who in our lives do we feel safe with—really safe, safe enough to open up about *everything*?

"Here is the promise of the gospel and the message of the whole Bible," Ortlund writes. "In Jesus Christ, we are given a friend who will always enjoy rather than refuse our presence. This is a companion whose embrace of us does not strengthen or weaken depending on how clean or unclean, how attractive or revolting, how faithful or fickle, we presently are. The friendliness of his heart for us subjectively is as fixed and stable as is the declaration of his justification of us objectively."

When I was in a particularly painful, solitary period in the midst of the global pandemic, I recall reading Ortlund's words and being reassured that this most important relationship—this most significant friend of all—continued to offer presence, peace, and provision. Christ, our ultimate friend, is fixed and stable no matter what.

Years ago, I sat with a small group of people attending a talk given by Brennan Manning. We listened to him speak with depth and gratitude on his savior's love for him and for us.

In his inimitable way Manning closed the talk with the words, "Don't should on yourself!" Several in the circle of friends erupted in laughter in recognition that we "should" on ourselves over and over again, and doing so is damaging to the soul. Like Ortlund, Manning reminded us that the Christ of the Gospels will always enjoy and never refuse the presence of his children, his followers. Our friendship with God will remain intact. On that, we can be assured.

～

The pavement that once carried the famed Route 66 from Chicago to Santa Monica, California, is a shell of its former self, replaced in large part by various Eisenhower Interstate System divided highways. But history enthusiasts keep the spirit of Route 66 alive with an annual Red Carpet Corridor Festival each May from Joliet to Towanda in Illinois along the path of the former highway. Midway on that ninety-mile festival route is the town of Dwight.

J. K., the pastor on the prairie, and I plan to make a visit to Ambler's Route 66 Texaco this year, and perhaps occupy a corner table at the Route 66 Diner for an extended, leisurely lunch. It's an unlikely place for a sustaining spiritual friendship and breaking bread with an *anam cara* friend. This soul friendship has now over time been forged in the promise and presence of friendship with Christ. Assured, promised. That friendship never moves away.

The Longing for Friendship
A Playlist

"Festival of Friends," Bruce Cockburn, from
the recording *Lord of the Starfields* (1976)

"(Get Your Kicks On) Route 66," Nat King Cole,
from the recording *The Nat King Cole Story* (1991)

"Lean On Me," Bill Withers, from
the recording *Still Bill* (1972)

"Friendship," Pops Staples, from the
recording *Don't Lose This* (2015)

"Count on Me," Bruno Mars, from the
recording *Doo-Waps & Hooligans* (2010)

"Isn't That What Friends Are For?," Bruce
Cockburn, from the recording *Breakfast in
New Orleans, Dinner in Timbuktu* (1999)

CHAPTER 9

The Longing for Meaningful Work

How do we come to choose what it is that we spend our days doing? Would we choose it again if we could? Did we choose it today, or has it simply carried us along somehow?

Robert Benson, *Between the Dreaming and the Coming True*

O ne of the annual end-of-year holiday traditions in my home over the better part of the past four decades has been our family's viewing of the 1946 film *It's a Wonderful Life*, directed and produced by Frank Capra and starring James Stewart as George Bailey and Donna Reed as his wife, Mary.

It's an unlikely holiday film in many ways, as much of it, though set largely on Christmas Eve, is actually quite dark and decidedly not filled with the merry making and good cheer we come to expect from our seasonal fare. A desperate man contemplating ending his own life by jumping off a bridge into the icy waters near the fictitious town of Bedford Falls on a snowy night doesn't exactly seem like must-see television as we welcome the Advent of Christ's glorious coming year after year. In fact, the film was not a commercial success upon its release, perhaps for that very reason, even as it garnered favorable critical reviews. Yet for many across the nation and the globe it's become an annual tradition. Why?

Among the varieties of its genius, Capra's film tapped into the deep longing we all hold to know our lives have had a positive impact on the world we inhabit; that our work, whatever that may be—a butcher, a baker, a candlestick maker, as the old nursery rhyme put it—has *mattered*. As the story of George Bailey's life is displayed in rewind and retold through the work of the self-proclaimed "angel, second-class," Clarence Oddbody, he realizes the ways in which his work at Bailey Building and Loan has had a purpose, a positive outcome. It has had *meaning*. Clarence also dramatically shows him what consequential, sad, grief-laden things would have happened to those in town, especially those who were immigrants, downtrodden, under the greed, power, and influence of Mr. Potter, if George had *not* been present in Bedford Falls for those many years prior to that fateful Christmas eve.

~

"I heard and I forgot. I saw and I remembered. I did and I understood."

Those were the words of promise that a group of faith-based fathers and their teenage sons and daughters wrapped themselves around at the picturesque ranch set in the mountains of northern California, a place for a week-long series of outdoor adventures and experiments in leadership. It was a line often repeated:

"I heard and I forgot. I saw and I remembered. I did and I understood."

During the day, campers rode the rapids of a nearby river in eight-person rafts, sailed down zip lines from high above a lake, competed in rope courses and other activities aimed at building community and self-confidence, and ate generous servings of food in the tents that served as a mess hall.

At night, as the youth gathered in their quarters, we fathers stayed up late talking about what brought us to the ranch and, invariably, what we left behind at home. We talked about our upbringings, our families.

And we talked about our work.

Most of the men who gathered nightly—doctors, dentists, lawyers, airline pilots, businessmen—were, it appeared, quite successful. But it was striking how so many who gathered in my lodge lamented the ways in which they spent their days.

Night after night I listened as they talked about the course their work had taken, the dreams they set aside, and the seeming waste of their lives. Not only did I hear in their words an echo of George Bailey's voice in the Capra film, but also heard a longing for their work to have a greater impact on others, to be more of an expression of their Christian faith, to be a source of greater meaning.

The conversation and the longing I heard brought to mind words from Annie Dillard's *The Writing Life*: "How we spend our days, of course, is how we spend our lives. What we do with this hour, and that one, is what we are doing." As I spoke with hesitancy about my own experience of work and the meaning I found inherent in it, I was peppered with questions and entered into dialogue about what constitutes meaningful work in a world in need.

Together we considered the unhelpfulness of the dualistic thinking about "sacred and secular" and how we make distinctions between "work and *full-time Christian* work"—as though one life were a diminishment and another sacred. Even as I considered those conversations, I held true gratitude for the trajectory of my own work life. With their voices echoing a yearning, I wanted to explore more fully the sources of my practical theology of work developed over more than four decades.

~

Scottish cleric Thomas Chalmers was also a philosopher and social reformer whose life traversed the eighteenth and nineteenth centuries. He's generally considered Scotland's greatest nineteenth-century church leader. It was said of him that the combination of immense drive with considerable charm formed Chalmers as a leader of the first magnitude.

In the primary biography of Chalmers, by Stewart J. Brown, the Scot was presented as both a practical social reformer with a clear agenda for the changes his nation needed and also a visionary who touched the lives and the conscience of the people of his time.

I first encountered Chalmers by reading Ben Patterson's book, *The Grand Essentials*. In it, Patterson quoted Thomas Chalmers as having said, "The grand essentials of happiness are: something to do, something to love, and something to hope for."

Just four years into my career in bookselling and publishing, I discovered Patterson's book. This former Presbyterian pastor and long-term college campus chaplain wrote with depth and wisdom, and the book has framed my approach to and my understanding of work ever since. I've read it so many times, the yellowed, marked-up paper is literally falling out of its binding and the book is held together by rubber bands.

For years until my supply ran out and couldn't be replenished, I gave a booklet-length excerpt of Patterson's book to every new employee I hired and asked them to read it and dialogue with me about it as part of their orientation to our work together. Patterson masterfully broke down the dichotomies that seemed to plague the lives of the men I talked to at that ranch long ago, and demonstrated the strong connection between our work and our worship of the living God:

- Something to do: our occupations (which we are paid for) and our vocations (which may or may not be what we derive income from)
- Something to love: God, our families, our friends, our neighbors, God's purposes in the world
- Something to hope for: ultimate restoration, reconciliation, shalom, all things being made right one day, some way

"We have to recover a sense of God's presence in our work in the world," Patterson writes. "But we won't until we recover a sense of his presence in the work we do in the sanctuary. God is as present in the liturgy of the world as in the liturgy of the sanctuary, but it is in worship that we tune our spirits to hear and see God amid the noise and bustle of work."

Is it possible, I wondered, that Patterson's thesis would have resonated in the hearts of those doctors and dentists, lawyers and airline pilots back at the ranch? Is it possible that tuning our spirits in worship would enable us to more fully see God amid the hum of their days at work? As I picked up the book with rubber bands holding it together, I thought that I, too, need to be reminded of that on a consistent basis.

In the years since first reading *The Grand Essentials* I've worked with Patterson on other writing projects and shared meals with him. In a recent conversation, he conveyed his late-career reflections on Chalmers's "grand essentials of happiness," distilling the guidance he would offer to any asking him for his insights today. Among the things he'd recommend:

- Seek to discern a sense of calling of what God has ordained each of us to do—which may or may not be what we're paid for.
- Pursue people who will walk with us in community as we journey on
- Find people with whom we can laugh

As I thought about those late-night lodge conversations, I considered questions worth my asking, our asking together, questions I wish I might have offered in that gathering: What have you discerned about your own vocation? With whom are you in community, to provide companionship and discernment on your journey? Who around you can you routinely laugh and enjoy light-hearted moments with in the midst of the warp and woof of the heaviness of life?

In *The Grand Essentials*, Patterson writes, "The hope of the resurrection is that, in Christ, my work will be raised with me; that somehow God will weave the frazzled threads of my life and work them into the great tapestry of salvation." Patterson goes on to say, "That hope delivers us from the despair that nothing we do matters, and enables us to tackle even the most menial job with vigor."

After reading *The Grand Essentials*, a new life was breathed into a passage in Colossians 3, becoming a guiding verse for my life and my work, whatever occupation I would hold: "Whatever you do, accomplish it from the soul, as to the Lord, and not to people, because you know that from the Lord you will receive the reward of the inheritance. Serve the Lord Christ" (vv. 23–24 Lexham English Bible).

As we long to live a life of meaning, and if our work occupies most of our waking hours, the importance of wrestling with occupational and vocational questions early and often, in community with others, is a wise course of action.

My own experience has mirrored and confirmed the simple yet wise guidance Patterson suggested in our conversation. While the majority of my adult life has been spent working with books and ideas—working with the life of the mind and the affections of the heart through published works—like most of us I've held a variety of occupations leading up to the time when I discovered the general contours of what I believed I was to do, what—in Patterson's words, God had *ordained* me to do.

In the course of my teens and early twenties, I baled hay on a rural farm, detasseled corn on hot summer days from the baskets of farm machinery, worked for many years as a cook at a steakhouse, and plugged solder into circuit boards on a factory assembly line. I spent a short season working as a sports editor of a small-town daily newspaper. With the benefit of hindsight, I see the ways in which all this work (and more that came after it) could be infused with meaning. I can also see how each of those roles impacted my determination to do something that tied into my passions and curiosities and what I was convinced was work that *needed* to be done in the world. And I had the help of others, the "community of people" who would walk with me on the journey.

A person who has wrestled as much and as deeply as anyone I know with questions of vocation and occupation is Steven Garber. He founded a not-for-profit called the Washington Institute for Faith, Vocation and Culture, designed to prompt reflection and understanding at the intersection of those three spheres, and he's written and spoken widely on the subject.

In his book *The Seamless Life*, Garber writes of the words *vocation* and *occupation* that, "The former is the longer, deeper story of someone's life, our longings and our choices and our passions that run through life like a deep river; the latter is what we do day by day, the relationships and responsibilities we occupy along the way of our lives, more like the currents in a river that give it visible form."

Using Garber's construct, my vocation—or the "deep river"—has flowed around the notion of being connected to bringing thoughtful ideas of impact into the world. The deep river has also been concerned with building bridges between individuals, teams, communities, and institutions. My occupation—the "currents in the river," in Garber's language—has taken many different forms, from bookseller, to publisher to writer, to trade association executive. Some of my deep river work has allowed me to make an income. A good portion of it has not. Yet all of it is my vocation, or calling, and God has been present in it, allowing the longing to be consistently cared for even in seasons of challenge, change, and confusion.

Along the way, I have had guides, mentors, and wise principles to follow—my metaphorical compass and cairns on the vocational trail.

∿

I have long enjoyed hiking, canoeing, or kayaking in the outdoors, far away from the bustle of cities and suburban sprawl and deeply into places where a canopy of stars (or, if one is fortunate on a late August night, the aurora borealis, or northern lights) shimmers in the darkened sky above. I relish going places where I need a compass in my hand and the assistance of cairns left behind by fellow travelers in order to find my way to the journey's destination.

Several years ago, on one such trip I read a book by Harvard Business School professor Bill George and Peter Sims of the Stanford Graduate School of Business titled *Discover Your True North*—an appropriate book to read in the wilderness!

In its pages, which were packed with principles on authentic leadership for people at all levels of organizations, I was instructed on the four points of what George and Sims label the compass for our work:

- *Values*—What are our most deeply held values? What principles guide our work?
- *Motivations*—What motivates us? How do we balance external and internal motivations?
- *Support Team*—Who are the people we can count on to guide and support and speak truth to us along the way?
- *Integrated Life*—How can we integrate all aspects of our life and find fulfillment?

When each part of the compass is well developed, George writes, we will be pointed toward our true north—toward what our lives and our work are all about. And we will be true to ourselves. In my work in the realm of Christian publishing, I'm witness to ways in which attending to these four points allows us to be faithful to our calling as believers in business.

Elsewhere in the book, George and Sims write,

There is no such thing as the instant leader. Your journey to authentic leadership will take you through many peaks and valleys as you encounter the world's trials, rewards and seductions. Becoming an authentic leader takes dedication to your development and growth, and there will be many temptations to pull you off the course of your True North. Maintaining your authenticity along the way may be the greatest challenge you ever face.

Regardless of whether or not you consider yourself a "leader" in the way George and Sims speak of, their guiding principles apply to all of us, our personhood as well, helping us derive meaning from our occupations and vocation. And whether we are young or old or something between, being open to new visions for our occupations and our vocation is renewing, a set of images that help us reevaluate our calling through new vision of gratitude, like George Bailey's set of images in rewind.

~

It's curious the way memories stay with us throughout our lives, clinging like kudzu vines on trees, abandoned homes, bridges, and other structures that dot the landscape of the southeastern United States.

Like the memory I carry with me of a desire to drive an eighteen-wheel truck for a living.

As a teenager I had no real inclination to attend a college or university and develop a pathway to a so-called professional career. There was no family pressure or expectation to do so, and few people on either side of my family system had pursued that route at the time. If there was any pressure, it was merely to ensure that I had a job that would provide for my needs as a young adult and allow me to move out of the family home at a proper time. While my friends began to think about what universities they would visit and apply to, I was dreaming of a very different way to spend my days and nights.

By the mid-'70s, the Penn Central railroad that long ran through my rural Midwest town had trimmed its timetables back substantially, with only one or two freight trains rumbling down the tracks daily. Passenger trains had not used the line for years. As I purchased my first car, a rust-over-white 1965 Ford Mustang, my treks down to the wooden trestle over Sugar Creek became less frequent, as were the afternoons and evenings sitting underneath its canopy reflecting and writing thoughts for an audience of none. With the benefit of a driver's license and time behind a steering wheel, my sights turned to a different mode of transportation to a new life, a different way to be in the world, a fresh pathway to move beyond the confines of my little town.

They turned to driving an eighteen-wheel Kenworth tractor trailer.

Perhaps I was influenced by my lack of travel beyond central Indiana. Most certainly I was influenced by a 1974–75 era NBC network television show called *Movin' On*, whose protagonists, Sonny Pruitt and Will Chandler, drove an eighteen-wheel tractor trailer across the country encountering adventures and solving mysteries. Whatever the case, I knew exactly what I wanted to do with my life:

Drive a semi-truck. An eighteen-wheel long hauler. The open road. Freedom. Adventure.

I might well have done that if not for the voice of a teacher, a diminutive Wisconsin native with the nickname Mo in honor of the early 1950s American tennis star Maureen Connolly. She became my version of the Richard Dreyfuss character in the film *Mr. Holland's Opus*, speaking wisdom, vision, and a modicum of self-confidence into a young life. While a life behind the wheel of a Kenworth semi may have been just fine for a life, I am now confident that, for me, my "Mr. Holland" was a voice I needed to hear, and heed.

That intersection with my teacher Mo is one I view as the real point of origin of my experience of a lifetime of meaningful work. She spoke profoundly into my life in ways that resonate to this day, though I have not seen her in decades. Her sense of what was possible pointed toward higher education. That, in turn, upon reflection on vocation and calling, led me to a life in the business of books, of ideas, of stories, of words. It led to a vocational calling centered on building bridges, publishing words, sharing books that built up others and ideas for the life of the mind and the affections of the heart. I trace even a recent late-career change, away from a long-term role in a single publishing house to something adjacent but very different, supporting the ways others bring books into the world, for the good of the world, back to the vision of vocation I was given all those years ago.

In an exploration on vocation that appears in a very personal work of spirituality, author Robert Benson asks a series of penetrating questions, relevant to all of us who long for the work we do to matter: "How do we come to choose what it is that we spend our days doing? Would we choose it again if we could? Did we choose it today, or has it simply carried us along somehow?"

For nearly four decades now, God has met the longing for meaningful work in a tangible way through my connections to Christian literature. Perhaps not unlike the registered nurse in a hospital, a financial adviser to prospective retirees, the teacher of young children, the youth minister or community development worker in the inner city, or a stay-at-home dad in the suburbs, I have seen the ways in which my work with words (principally supporting and publishing others') has an impact on the lives of other people who engage with ideas, have their biases challenged through a resource placed in their hands, or consider alternative points of view.

"We spend our days doing what we do for all kinds of reasons. It is the work we have been given to do or what we have found to do. Some of us do work that seems to have found us in some way, for better or worse," Benson writes in his wise book *Between the Dreaming and the Coming True.* "A fair number of us do things that we love to do, whatever that might mean to us, but if you ask very many people if that is so for them, not as many of them will say yes as you might have thought or hoped."

When we find ourselves at crossroads, wondering about the sense of longing we have for greater meaning in our vocations and our occupations, the four points of our compass help us reexamine and assess where we are:

- Have our values changed?
- Do we need to reconsider our motivations for how we are spending our days?
- What is our support team (our mentors, spiritual friends) telling us?
- Are there aspects of our life that are "divided" (see chapter 2) and in need of reintegration?

Parker Palmer, whose seminal work *Let Your Life Speak* formed my understanding of work and calling, has written, "Vocation at its deepest level is, 'This is something I can't not do, for reasons I am unable to explain to anyone else and don't fully understand myself but that are nonetheless compelling.'" It is when we are in *that* bedrock place that we are most likely to recognize the meaning in what we are doing, how we are spending our days, and why.

~

At the end of the cherished "holiday" classic, of course, George Bailey, the man who that same day felt like all was lost—his life, his home, that all would better without him—is met with the unexpected, showered with words of affection from the joyful residents of Bedford Falls, and given donations to cover the eight thousand dollars in missing funds the bank examiner required to prevent turning the Bailey bank over to the evil, dark-hearted Mr. Potter. As the film winds to a close, the bell on the Baileys' Christmas tree rings out, and George's daughter Zuzu explains that somewhere, an angel just received its wings.

And George received metaphorical wings too. He was reminded of the wonderful life he had led and the meaning inherent in it. What was once lost—his *saudade*—was found.

The Longing for Meaningful Work
A Playlist

"Fast Car," Tracy Chapman, from the recording *Tracy Chapman* (1988)

"It's My Job," Livingston Taylor, from the recording *The Middle Years* (1991)

"Working on a Dream," Bruce Springsteen, from the recording *Working on a Dream* (2009)

"Mr. Tanner," Harry Chapin, from the recording *Short Stories* (1974)

"Trouble in the Fields," Nanci Griffith with the London Symphony Orchestra, from *The Dust Bowl Symphony* (1999)

"Cleaning Windows," Van Morrison, from the recording *Beautiful Vision* (1982)

PART III

OUR ETERNAL LONGINGS

The Christian vision of heaven affirms that what the psalmist longed for all his life will one day be the common privilege of the entire people of God—to gaze upon the face of their Lord and Savior, as they enter into his house, to dwell in peace forever.

Alister E. McGrath

CHAPTER 10

The Longing for Heaven

I believe heaven is the home that awaits us at the end of our journey. We are all trying to make our way home, and God leads us there by placing road signs for us along the way.

Christopher de Vinck, *Finding Heaven*

It was a bright autumn day, the kind of Saturday tailor-made for college football on American university campuses or soccer matches in other parts of the world. Preparations among a group of friends and I were well underway to walk the two miles from our dormitories to the university's stadium, beverages and blankets in tow, to watch an early-season game between two mediocre mid-major conference teams. But a call to my dorm room changed those light-hearted plans.

It changed a whole lot more than watching a football game.

It was the kind of call that shocked a young life and nearly unraveled a still-unformed faith. In words few in number but packed with deep grief, I was told that Alex, a friend who just five years before had introduced me to the hope he'd found in embracing religious faith as a follower of Christ, had died by suicide. Alex, who had eagerly led me along the path of faith through the gift of a small paperback book, *Me, Be Like Jesus?*, a paraphrased copy of the New Testament, and through his exhortation about God's plan for my life, was gone.

Questions swirled in my mind as I drove home, unsure what I would find or how to act in the presence of Alex's family, whom I would soon see. The age-old "why?" questions associated with the deaths of the young rode along with me as I made my way past the agricultural fields of the rural Midwest that sunny morning, as well as never-before-experienced questions related to *this kind* of death. Bewilderment over why the very person who had told me in vivid detail and with passion about faith, about the assurance of eternity in heaven, and about God's purposes for my life on earth had taken his own life, also rode with me that day. *Was it all just make-believe, this hope? Was I naïve to join my friend on this journey? Where is God in this? Why didn't God intervene? Didn't God have a plan for Alex's life on earth?*

At the time, I had no understanding of the complexities of mental health or brain chemistry. I had no knowledge of or personal experience with depression then as I do now. I knew nothing of the depth of grief that my friend's family members and those closest to them were dealing with in death's immediate aftermath (and would continue to deal with in some way for the remainder of their lives). I simply knew the person who had shared the first life-giving message about Christian hope I'd ever heard—and did so at a key point in my midteen years—was now gone, and I was at a loss to understand why it had happened.

"While suicides often take place in isolation, they are never unnoticed by others," Albert Y. Hsu, whose father died by suicide, writes in *Grieving a Suicide*, a book that seeks to bring comfort, hope, and answers to survivors of suicide. "There may be one primary victim, but as with a bomb thrown into a crowd of people, the collateral damage done to others nearby is massive."

The collateral damage for Alex's family was significant, and for a period of time my faith was shaken to the core. That Christian faith, which for the preceding five years had begun to take shape in a haphazard, halting, but real way for the first time in my life, initially prompted by Alex, was inextricably connected to a person who was now gone. A melancholia set in. In that period, questions of heaven and hell took on new and unsettling dimensions.

~

This book began by exploring our longing for home and acknowledged that our search for home is deeply rooted in our humanity. The sense of homesickness many of us carry throughout our lives may indeed be pointing us toward our heart's true home, heaven. C. S. Lewis seems to offer this idea in his classic work *Mere Christianity* when, amid the calamity of World War II, he went on a British Broadcasting Corporation (BBC) radio program and said, "If I find in myself a desire which no experience in this world can satisfy, the most probable explanation is that I was made for another world."

The longing for heaven, the final chapter in our journey together, is unique among the ten topics addressed in the pages of this book, as the Portuguese understanding and experience of *saudade* is decidedly attached to things we *genuinely once knew*—something or someone real in our past that we long to see, to know, to enjoy once again. And despite the often fanciful messages we sometimes read in popular books or online articles written by or about people who claim they have visited the afterlife and returned to tell us about it in vivid detail, heaven is normally seen as something in our future. Thus, it's inappropriate to connect *saudade* to heaven in the same way as to home, peace, forgiveness, friendship, or any of the other topics I have addressed.

Yet the longing for heaven creeps into the hearts and minds of those of us who wish to live an attentive life, perhaps especially as we age and are confronted with the reality of decline and the end-of-life questions we try to keep at bay as long as we can. Over the past year, my mother and I have had repeated conversations about the topic as she has faced one illness after another, each one sapping her strength but paradoxically fortifying her resolve. On the other end of the spectrum, the notion of heaven is present in the words of evangelists, with their voices raised in heated, impassioned warnings, telling us of the eternal fires that await the person separated from the saving grace of Christ. It envelops us as we struggle to cope with the loss of a child, whom we hope to see on the "other side" somewhere, some day. This longing visits us when severe illness or disability arises and we wish for the return of the fully abled body we once knew, and we wonder if it will be so in heaven. It bangs on the door of our hearts and minds when a beloved friend takes his or her own life and we ask, as I did that sunny Saturday morning, "*Why? How? What now?*"

The longing for heaven rushes into our hearts and minds when we face the death of an aged loved one, as I did on that December morning when my father drew his last breath just as the Brahms lullaby played, welcoming a new birth in the nearby maternity ward of the hospital—an ending, a beginning, a mystery.

Perhaps that is the most appropriate word attached to this eternal longing . . . this longing for heaven: mystery.

And perhaps that is as it should be.

~

Throughout much of my adult life I have striven for certainty, for answers, for solutions to the doubts and questions I've encountered internally and externally:

- About God
- About Scripture
- About myself
- About the world around me
- About interfaith issues

- About what constitutes right and wrong and how we know
- About ethics
- About the church

Questions related to these and other subjects regularly appear, demanding to be acknowledged and dealt with. My search for answers has been prompted, I believe, by a need to build a solid, ironclad framework that offered at least the *perception* of certainty and safety from the chaos and unbounded life I'd often felt as a young person—and, if I'm honest, that I carry with me still, in some measure and some seasons.

Recently in preparation for a job change that would have me working from a small, home-based office, I was forced to trim down the space allotted to my personal and professional library. I gave away hundreds of volumes I'd amassed in nearly four decades of work in bookselling and publishing. As I handled each book over the course of a month making decisions about which ones stayed and which were given away, I could see the trajectory of questions I had in my twenties, thirties, forties, and fifties and the sources I looked to as I sought the certainty I felt would build a good and faithful life.

Questions both serious and simply silly curiosities about heaven have stymied me, however, questions like the following:

- Where is heaven?
- Who will be there?
- Is there family in heaven?
- Is there marriage?

- Is heaven composed of continual worship?
- Are the fanciful angels and harps *really* a part of the deal?
- What about bodies? Are they as we'd known them on earth?
- Will there be baseball?
- What about our beloved pet?
- What about . . . ?

The questions, both serious and light-hearted, are endless, as are the mysteries in response.

Like most people I know, I do long for heaven. The older I've gotten, the more top of the mind it has become and the more I find myself wanting to know what it will *really* mean. But it now comes with a question mark: Is a granular level of certainty even possible in response to this longing? Perhaps even more than our longings for home, friendship, transformation, and other longings of the heart, heaven is something we must embrace as a mystery. Maybe we allow that to be good enough, trusting in a trustworthy God, and trustworthy Scriptures, and traditions handed down through the centuries.

A recent book titled *The Case for Heaven* by Lee Strobel moves largely in the opposite direction of mystery, investigating broad questions in journalistic fashion for evidence regarding life after death, an approach he has taken with prior works on miracles, Christ, creation, and grace. In it, he powerfully tells the story of his friend Nabeel, who was afflicted with stomach cancer and died at the age of thirty-four. Reflecting on all he had learned in his journalistic search for answers on the afterlife, Strobel wrote, "Yes, heaven means hope—not a vapid kind of wishful thinking or a cross-your-fingers sort of blind optimism, but a confident hope. I trust I will be reunited with my friend Nabeel someday—and the persuasive evidence for the resurrection and the reality of heaven tells me that my trust is indeed well placed."

Although there is a cottage industry of books on the topic of heaven, my experience suggests that in our society, our churches, homes, and among friends, it's not something we talk about a great deal. It's not even something the Bible speaks of with as much concrete imagery or declarations as other topics. The New International Version lists 422 uses of *heaven* or *heavens*. More often than not, when the word is used in Scripture it's speaking of "the heavens" connected to creation stories in Genesis. John's Revelation, of course, depicts aspects of heaven with vivid imagery that makes readers of the text want to understand Greek in order to have more confidence that we are interpreting it correctly. Paul's first epistle to the church in Corinth talks extensively and with great confidence about not only the resurrection of Christ but also the resurrection of the dead and the resurrection body (see 1 Corinthians 15), which is comforting. But for me, the language and imagery in the Bible related to heaven is an intersection of confusing elements.

A group of scholars who collected a major reference book on the imagery of Scripture write in their entry on heaven, "The imagery used to portray heaven is a mingling of the familiar and the unfamiliar, the earthly and the more-than-earthly. Heaven is a place, but not exactly like earthly places. It contains recognizable features, but the motifs of strangeness and transcendence keep alive our awareness that earthly images do not exist in the ordinary manner in heaven."

Strangeness and transcendence. Again, mystery.

New Testament professor Scot McKnight's take on heaven acknowledges mystery but is delightfully refreshing as he examines the many reasons he believes this eternal longing is and can be a reality for us. In *The Heaven Promise*, McKnight distinguishes between two senses regarding heaven in the Bible—what he calls a "present heaven" with a lowercase *h* and "a final kingdom of God, a future Heaven" with an uppercase *H*.

With conviction and passion, McKnight says that the "single most important fact the Bible teaches about heaven is this: God has promised Heaven. If Heaven is God's promise, then Heaven is as good as God is faithful."

McKnight goes on to give his personal statement of belief in heaven, which centers around nine specific truths he sees in the Bible and the Christian tradition, including things we would expect from a New Testament professor: the belief in Christ and the early apostles, the resurrection of Jesus, and the Bible's comment on the subject. But two others on his list are surprising and arresting: beauty and grandeur in the world, and desire implanted in human persons.

To the particulars of Scripture and Christian tradition I bring intellectual assent, I bring faith that "heaven is as good as God is faithful." Yet I hold something within that is mystery: beauty and desire undergird my own longing for heaven, even as they further shape my trust in its reality.

~

Christopher de Vinck, in his book *Finding Heaven: Stories of Going Home*, writes that we "believe heaven is the home that awaits us at the end of our journey. We are all trying to make our way home, and God leads us there by placing road signs for us along the way."

McKnight's notion of beauty in particular resonates with me as a road sign in our journey toward heaven, our heart's true home. I recall canoeing Lac la Croix on the Canadian side of the Boundary Waters Canoe Area for seven days. After catching fish (with the help of a First Nations Chippewa guide) and cooking our meal on the shore of a small island, I watched as a majestic bald eagle, with its snow-white head and dark brown feathered body, descended and lifted the remains of the walleye we just a short time before had caught, now held in its talons. The eagle soared overhead to destinations unknown, poised to partake of what was left of our catch, the skeleton of the walleye dangling through the air.

I was awestruck by the beauty of this massive bird in flight, the crystalline water and jack pine, balsam fir, and white spruce trees all around me. I remember saying to myself amid the silence, "The wonders of creation beg for all the world to see." It was in some transcendent way beauty's reassurance of heaven. I've read about the thin places of Ireland or the Scottish island of Iona, and I've traveled to that part of the world and had a taste of what that means. But it was in Lac la Croix at the end of that shoreline luncheon that I most sensed a thin place, a powerful reassurance of the Creator's presence, love, and a place of eternal life, even amid the mystery.

It is one of the ways God has met me in this longing.

In his book *A Brief History of Heaven*, British theologian Alister McGrath hints at this experience when he writes, "The longing for heaven that is evoked by nature is held to rest on the anticipation of seeing the creator of the world, who may be dimly glimpsed through the wonders of the created order."

Echoes of heaven in the natural world are not the only road sign marked by beauty on the way.

Throughout the pandemic that gripped our world and led to the loss of an enormous number of lives and to isolation such as few of us had known before, the renowned cellist Yo-Yo Ma began recording and posting videos as part of the Songs of Comfort Project. In an interview with the journalist Jeffrey Brown on the *PBS News Hour*, Yo-Yo Ma was asked what motivated him to undertake the project.

"It came to me spontaneously," he told Brown. "I was in my office and said, 'Let's do something in this time that actually serves people's needs. Music has always been comforting to me. This is what I do. And this is the best that I can offer." As the interview with Brown concluded, Yo-Yo Ma took his cello in hand and played Antonín Dvořák's "Goin' Home" from *Symphony No. 9*.

Week after week throughout the pandemic, this cellist's
songs of comfort posted on social media fortified people
throughout the world. And for me, they instilled a longing
for heaven, a "goin' home" not unlike what is evoked in his
performance of Dvórak's piece. They were moments of alignment, and signposts on the way.

"In heaven what we want and what we have will be per-
fectly aligned," writes Mark McMinn in *Finding Our Way
Home*. "Today, as we live in our broken world, the alignment
is never quite right. It's like turning the focus ring on a camera, trying to bring the camera into perfect focus but never
getting it exactly correct. But someday all will be in focus—
our desires and our environment in perfect adjustment."

I remember once sitting with Mark as together we listened
to a Fernando Ortego song titled "Beyond the Sky," a contemporary composition that captured with profound imagery
a moment "when time is done and bright heaven will be our
refuge." It was a moment of beauty *and* desire colliding and
very nearly bringing that focus ring into perfect alignment,
with a portrait of heaven. It was a moment of God meeting
us both in this longing.

Georgia-born folk artist and composer Brooks Williams
years ago performed at a private booksellers event I was a
part of. In his set he included a song that has since that time
become a touchstone in my longing for heaven: "We Will
Dance Someday." In it Williams combines both beauty and
desire in a single, four-minute composition. It evokes my Lac
la Croix experience, and articulates my hopes for heaven.

Far from the mad crowd
Where you can hear yourself think out loud
And you can breathe the smokeless air
Drink deep of the silence for it's there
We will dance someday

Beneath a canopy of stars
Stretching bright both near and far
Smell the trees, hear the lake water lap
Soak it in and begin there's no turning back
We will dance someday

When the last tear has been cried
And death and disease have died
We can turn and we can finally embrace
Find that peace for this human race

When the sky in the East turns red
And the mountains begin to crack
When the last jet plane has flown
The Lord of the Dance will take us home.
We will dance someday.

I think of my friend Alex when I hear "We Will Dance Some-day." I long to see him dancing in heaven, to join him in that dance and in drinking in silence and knowing that the last tear has been cried, that death has died, and we have all made our way to our hearts' true home.

The Longing for Heaven
A Playlist

"We Will Dance Someday," Brooks Williams,
from the recording *North from Statesboro* (1989)

"Heaven/Where True Love Goes," Yusuf,
from the recording *An Other Cup* (2006)

"Can I Go with You," Bruce Cockburn, from
the recording *Further Adventures Of* (1978)

"Heaven," Los Lonely Boys, from the
recording *Los Lonely Boys* (2004)

"Beyond the Sky," Fernando Ortega,
from the recording *Home* (2000)

"Goin' Home," Antonín Dvórak's *Symphony
No. 9*, from the Yo-Yo Ma and Kathryn Scott
recording *Songs of Comfort and Hope* (2020)

EPILOGUE

> We are people of desire. We want things. We long
> for things. It is primal to our nature to yearn. As Saint
> Augustine reflected, "The whole life of the good
> Christian is a holy longing. . . . That is our life, to be
> trained by longing."
>
> **Curt Thompson,** *The Soul of Desire*

I've spent much of my adult life trying to arrive at a clear
and consistent understanding of the relationship between
desire and discipleship; between ambition and humility;
between freedom and obedience. The road I've traveled has
been, in the words of Paul McCartney, a long and winding
one, decidedly not straight and narrow. Winds of change
come with increasing regularity and intensity and cause the
questions to arise anew.

Many of the questions I've wrestled with in my own heart
and mind over many years, and the ponderings in response,
have emerged in these pages as I've considered ten distinct
longings that I believe are clearly of God in my life, longings

in which the relational triune God of grace has met me, and has perhaps met you as well.

The spirituality writer and pastor Jeffrey Tacklind has written that the path of transformation is a winding road filled with equal parts glory and humility. Reading about that path, I resonated with that assertion and feel it's true for most of us. Tacklind writes,

> Ever since I was a child, I've longed to live a life of nobility and glory. In every adventure story I was caught up in, or hero's biography I digested, there was the underlying question: *Could this be me?* I longed to live a glorious story. But this longing has always been held in check by a more cautious, but no less virtuous voice, telling me to beware my pride and self-conceit—that part of me that would quickly rise up in moments of triumph and contaminate them with my own fantasies and self-indulgence and aggrandizement. These two longings have forever created tension in the deepest places of my heart. A battle for both glory and humility.

I love his recognition of a lifetime of tension. My experience of the spiritual life has, like Tacklind's, had a lifelong tension in deep recesses of my heart, but not just around the poles of nobility and humility. Additionally, I have sensed tension between desire and discipleship, ambition and selfishness, the self and the other, suffering and beauty.

Like many Christians, for me the idea that it's not only permissible but *good* for us to be in touch with our desires—our longings—was for a long time a vexing proposition. Aren't we

to deny ourselves? Isn't being in touch with these things opening the door to self-preoccupation? Isn't it risking selfishness,
real or perceived?

And yet we carry these desires, our deepest longings, with us.
It's part of what it means to be human, and they are drivers in
our lives whether or not we acknowledge them. They're among
our most powerful drivers. In discernment, it's important to ask
questions about our longings, questions like, "Is this longing of
God? Does it draw me in the direction of truth, beauty, and
goodness? Does it make me a more whole, more integrated,
more loving, more wholehearted person? Or does it direct me
in the way of a divided life, away from God, and away from
others with whom I share important, life-giving ties?"

Three distinct elements of my life have guided my own
discernment about the longings I carry with me, and through
which I desire to meet the God of grace, all of which dot
the pages of *The Language of the Soul.* The written word in
journals, prayer books, literature, poetry and especially the
Psalms; music, whether instrumental or with vocals, classical
or folk, jazz or popular; and the natural world, which is my
most common site in which to practice Ignatius's examen.

The natural world, especially places at a significant distance
from crowds where silence is truly possible, offers a path of
reflection and contemplation that prompts connecting to the
stirrings and longings of the soul.

Places like Glendalough in Ireland.

On two occasions I have made a journey to Glendalough in
County Wicklow, on the eastern coast of the island. It's the site of
one of the most well-preserved ancient monastic communities

in Ireland, founded by St. Kevin in the early seventh century. Two stunning lakes reside on upper and lower portions of the glacial valley, as does the well-preserved St. Kevin's Church, the ruins of Trinity Church a short walk away from the central portion of the community, and an iconic round tower. Located within the Wicklow National Park, "Glendalough has attracted pilgrims and visitors over many centuries for its hallowed surroundings, its traditions and its stunning scenery," an interpretive sign reads. "A remarkable collection of ruined medieval churches is spread out over 3km along the valley. As a relatively unaltered group of up to nine Romanesque or earlier churches, it is unique in Ireland and Britain."

On a solo journey to Glendalough, I carried with me the UK edition of the book *Benedictus*, a collection of blessings by the late poet and priest John O'Donohue, who was born in County Clare, Ireland, and whose work is deeply connected to the land and the longings of the people who have resided there. One of the blessings I read that day on the shores of the Upper Lake of Glendalough (shared below) was his "For Longing":

For Longing

A Blessing by John O'Donohue (1956–2008)

Blessed be the longing that brought you here
And quickens your soul with wonder.

May you have the courage to listen to the voice of
desire
That disturbs you when you have settled for something safe.

May you have the wisdom to enter generously into
  your own unease
To discover the new direction your longing wants
  you to take.

May the forms of your belonging—in love, creativ-
  ity, and friendship
Be equal to the grandeur and the call of your soul.

May the one you long for long for you.

May your dreams gradually reveal the destination of
  your desire.

May a secret providence guide your thought and
  nurture your feeling.

May your mind inhabit your life with the sureness
  with which your body inhabits the world.

May your heart never be haunted by ghost-structures
  of old damage.

May you come to accept your longing as divine
  urgency.

May you know the urgency with which God longs
  for you.

The closing words of O'Donohue's blessing may well be the most essential truth I have discovered on the pilgrimage of life thus far. God the Father, Son, and Spirit does, in truth, long for me, for you, for all of humankind. This God longs for us also to know and embrace a path of forgiveness, peace, friendship, transformation, community, and meaningful work as longings that bring us with "divine urgency," near to the heart of God. Our routes will be unique. Our roads will be long and winding. But we are guided along this camino by one who knows and loves us as children of great worth.

And one day, we will be home.

Epilogue
A Playlist

"Glendalough," Carl Lord, from the recording *Stillness* (2001)

"Heaven Ain't Ready for Me Yet," Emmylou Harris, from the recording *Portraits* (1996)

"Shenandoah," the Chieftains, from the recording *The Essential Chieftains* (2006)

"Knockin' on Heaven's Door," Bob Dylan, from the recording *Pat Garrett and Billy the Kid* (1973)

"The Shores of the Swilly," Phil Coulter, from the recording *Lake of Shadows* (2001)

"Glendalough," Innisfree, from the recording *Celtic Dreams* (1999)

AFTERWORD

James Bryan Smith

Recently my daughter, Hope, played a game with me using her iPhone and a Bluetooth speaker. She pulled up a playlist of pop songs from the 1970s and asked me to try to "Name That Tune." She would play a few seconds of a song and see how long it would take me to name the song *and* the name of the band or singer. I was astonished at how many of these songs were lodged in my mind. I answered about nine out of ten songs in only a few bars, sometimes even just a few notes. Then something else came over me: the memories surrounding those songs. Each song came with a memory, a time in my younger days when those songs were not "oldies" but very much a part of the soundtrack of my life.

With each memory came a feeling of longing. Many of the songs sparked memories of important times in my life. "That song was playing when I drove my own car for the first time." "That song was played over and over at the summer swimming pool, when I had my first crush." "We played that song in the locker room before every game." I remembered people and felt feelings and longed for those days and those people. A year later I went to my fortieth high school reunion, and saw many of those same faces I saw in the songs, now older, grayer, more wrinkly, but the same souls they were when we wore bell bottoms and thought we were cool.

A couple of years ago some of my close friends threw a party in my honor. People I know and love, people who mean a great deal to me, all shared their own stories about me and the work I have done and how much they appreciate me. In a world where we get a lot of rejection and criticism, this affirmation was incredibly gratifying. Then a video was played, and it featured Jeff Crosby, the author of this wonderful book. Jeff spoke movingly about how we met, about our friendship, and what my writing had meant to him. Jeff's words brought me to tears. It was a night to remember, and it filled me with great joy. It was too much for me to take in.

But in truth, it also left me feeling as if something was missing, a longing for something more. How could this be? This was one of the best moments of my life, and yet I still felt as if it were incomplete.

Not long ago I gave a talk about grief, and about hope. In my talk I shared memories of people in my life who had died—my soul friend, the singer-songwriter Rich Mullins, my daughter, Madeline, my mother, and my mentor, Dallas Willard. I spoke about the hope of heaven, about how deep within me was a yearning to see them well, to see them again, in our eternal home. With each person I recalled who had gone on to glory came a feeling of longing. Memories of their laughter filled with a yearning to see them again combined to create a deep feeling within me that I could not describe. A longing for the past and a longing for the future all at the same time. In those '70s songs I felt a longing about something in my past, at the celebration put together by my friends I felt a longing for something in the present, and in my grief I felt a longing for something in the future.

I could not name those longings. Until now.

This deeply personal and well-written book finally gave me the words to describe this longing, this yearning, this deep desire that, while still a mystery, is captured in the Portuguese word *saudade*.

I have been to Brazil three times, and I learned firsthand about the importance of this word to those who speak the language. As Jeff mentions, whenever I asked my Brazilian brothers and sisters about the word *saudade*, there was always a pause, and a misty-eyed look, as they tried to tell me what the word means. And then they always said, "But we do not expect you to understand it." And they were right. But now I think I do understand it. And I now see how *pervasive* this longing, this *saudade* is for all people.

Reading the book gave me many gifts, but one of the best ones is the sense that I am not alone in my longings. As I read, I was also reminded of a talk I heard, by Chris Webb, about the Welsh word *hiraeth*. The people of Wales, Chris said, love this word because it expresses nostalgia, homesickness, and longing all at the same time. *Hiraeth* has been called "the untranslatable word that connects Wales." In reading this book it hit me—this mysterious, untranslatable feeling is something we *all* have. All people. At all times. Everywhere.

Now I have a better sense not only of what the word means, but what it means for each us, and how it connects us to God and to one another.

I am so grateful for this book and for Jeff and his courage and honesty and skill in how he has written it. I am grateful that he tells such vivid and personal stories from his own life, confessional and insightful, stories that resonate and reveal these deep inner longings that we all have—longings for peace and forgiveness and community, to name a few. I believe these inner desires are *factory loaded* into our souls when we are born. We cannot escape them, and we cannot fulfill these needs with the things of this earth. Since Jeff is a great musicologist and aficionado, I can only appeal to U2 *and* to Rich Mullins to explain it: "I still haven't found what I'm looking for. . . . But everywhere I go, I'm looking."

And I cannot stop the longing or the looking. And that is good.

I loved every chapter, but I have to admit that I found myself most drawn to and inspired by chapter 2, on the longing for an undivided life. Jeff quotes some of my favorite writers, some whom I have known and met—Frederick Buechner, Parker Palmer, Brennan Manning, and Henri Nouwen. But what Jeff has done in this masterful chapter is to unlock something they were all trying to say but I had failed to grasp. Using insights like *consolation* and *desolation* and *integration* helps explain how the "wall," as Palmer put it, between my inner and outer life, between my onstage and backstage self (both artificial constructs, by the way), began to disappear like the Möbius strip exercise Jeff talks about in the book.

And it warmed my heart and created a desire to live as integrated as I can.

One quote in particular took hold of me, as, I suppose, it had done so to Jeff (writers love to write about what grasps them). The quote is from Parker Palmer: "I can't imagine any more satisfying way to go out than to be able to say to the best of my ability in the work I did and the relationships I held . . . that I was there as who I am, I was there with my best gifts. . . . I was there honestly and truly and real." I love it when not just a quote, but a whole book grabs me and ignites within me a longing I have always had but did not have the words to describe. I am grateful to Jeff Crosby for giving all of us these wonderful words. I will treasure this book for the rest of my life.

QUESTIONS FOR PERSONAL REFLECTION AND GROUP DISCUSSION

T*he following questions tied to each of the ten chapters of this book are designed for use either by individuals or small groups who may be studying together in community.*

Chapter 1: The Longing for Home

- What and where constitutes "home" for you? Dwell on that image of home. What were its sights? Its smells? Who were the people that surrounded you? Who and what was or is now important to you?
- Take a moment and journal your reflections in response to what you have surfaced about your images and memories of home. What are these memories trying to say to you?
- How is this longing for home, for you, a foreshadowing of what you have been taught about the concept of heaven?

Chapter 2: The Longing for an Undivided Life

- How would you define an "integrated" or "an undivided" life?
- Reflect on your experience of barriers to an undivided life. What have they been and what was the impact?
- What spiritual practices have you found helpful in cultivating an integrated life?

Chapter 3: The Longing for Freedom from Fear and Anxiety

- Take a moment to consider the shape your experience of fearfulness or perhaps anxiety has taken. What stands out to you?
- In times of significant fear and anxiety, how have you navigated its effects on your well-being? What spiritual practices have guided you toward hope and peace?
- What role might proper rest play in helping us?

Chapter 4: The Longing for Forgiveness

- Take time to journal on your own experience of receiving (or desiring) the forgiveness of God. What are the elements of that story? How did the story end, or what is still being written?
- Reflect on a time when forgiveness was extended to you in a significant and life-giving way. How did that feel to you? What light did that bring to your soul?

- Lewis Smedes has written that some believe forgiving ourselves—or "solitaire forgiveness"—makes as much sense as one-person tennis. What is your view of the efficacy and necessity of the art of forgiving ourselves? How have you experienced self-forgiveness?

Chapter 5: The Longing for Spiritual Transformation

- What narratives have you carried with you about the notion of spiritual change or transformation throughout your journey of faith? Which have brought light and life? Which, if any, have brought the opposite?
- The image of the jack pine and its reliance on fire is suggested as a metaphor for spiritual transformation. What has your experience of metaphorical fire and its relationship to spiritual transformation or formation been?
- The author suggests that metaphorical heat is not the only vehicle for spiritual transformation. What are other spiritual practices that have led to transformation in your experience?

Chapter 6: The Longing for Peace

- Take a journal and pen in hand and respond to the question, "When have you recently felt most at peace?" What did you reflect on and write in your journal? What made that moment or that season filled with peace?

• What aspects of peace do you yearn for in your own life, your community, your world?

• What is your experience of having peace with God? Describe your pathway.

Chapter 7: The Longing for Community

• When you hear the words *community* or *Christian community*, what is evoked in your own spirit? What do you immediately think of?

• How have you experienced community in your life? What have the costs and graces been for you?

• Who has modeled for you the very best of community? What about them made it such a positive example? How have you incorporated that example into your own experiences of community?

Chapter 8: The Longing for Friendship

• Reflect on or journal about the state of friendships in your own life. What words or phrases emerge?

• With whom have you experienced spiritual friendships or *anam cara*–like friendships? Reflect and journal on the history of those relationships—how they began and were nurtured. What emerges in your heart and mind?

• How do you respond to Dane Ortlund's suggestion in this chapter that Christ offers us a vertical relationship, "a friend who will always enjoy rather than refuse our presence"? How does that promise correspond to your experience?

Chapter 9: The Longing for Meaningful Work

- Take time to reflect on and journal about the variety of jobs you've occupied in your lifetime. From which of them did you derive the most joy, satisfaction, and meaning? What about those roles or locations made that so?
- How has your view of work changed over time? What aspects, if any, have remained consistent throughout your life?
- Author and chaplain Ben Patterson contends that work is a blessing and not a curse, and that work is essential to our humanness. He contends that the Bible even makes the assertion that to work is to do a godlike thing. What is your perspective? What about your own journey has formed that view?

Chapter 10: The Longing for Heaven

- Reflect on and journal about the images or teaching on heaven that you've received throughout your life. What stands out most significantly? What among those images or teachings has brought comfort? What, if anything, attached to it has brought fear?
- What has influenced your views of heaven over time? How has it changed?

- Though the Bible does speak about the promise of heaven, it's a subject cloaked in mystery for those of us on this side of the veil. How have you seen others close to you who have neared the end of their lives approach this mystery and promise? How do you think of it yourself today?

GRATITUDES

Books more often than not carry the name of a single person on their covers, but *all* books are the product of a community of people who lift their writers and messages up in some way: family members who give up time with the author as they research, reflect, and write; friends who read early drafts and offer constructive critique and words of encouragement in equal measure; and editors and publishers who take words on a page, shape and sharpen them, and carry the end product out into the world. The following people are among the members of my community who have helped make *The Language of the Soul* a reality:

Suzanne Stabile and James Bryan Smith, writers in spiritual formation and spirituality, have through their books and their friendship contributed significantly to my understanding of the life of faith. Thank you both for your words contained in this manuscript. Even more so, thank you for your imprint on my life.

Joaquim Fragoso, a native of Brazil and a former colleague, has taught me much about *saudade*, for which I'm deeply grateful. Even more so, Joaquim, thank you for your example of faithfulness, servanthood, and joy even in the midst of sorrow.

To René Breuel, a native of Brazil, and to Mark Carpenter, chairman and CEO of Editora Mundo Cristão in São Paulo, Brazil, thank you for offering feedback on my earliest *saudade* reflections and questions as I sought to ensure acceptable appropriation of a word that is so meaningful in your culture. I'm grateful to both of you and to Joaquim for that. Any remaining misuse, of course, I take responsibility for.

To J. K. Jones, my pastor-on-the-prairie soul friend. I'm grateful for your spiritual friendship and direction in my life. I look forward to our next meal together along Route 66 in Dwight!

Sharon Garlough Brown, your gift of listening, *truly* hearing, and responding with words of truth, hope, and healing are a gift both in your writing and in your friendships and spiritual direction in the lives of people like me.

Rita Hassert of the Sterling Morton Library in Lisle, Illinois, was an invaluable help with my research on the jack pine and the Belmont Prairie. Our family's long-term friend Betty Hodge provided a helpful limited-edition published history of London, Indiana for the chapter on home.

Dr. Sherry Rediger and Dr. Margaret Wehrenberg read early drafts of the chapter on fear and anxiety and offered helpful feedback borne out of their respective practices. I extend my gratitude to you both for your professional expertise. Likewise, Christine Marie Eberle, a gifted writer of spirituality books and a long-time campus chaplain, read an early version of the manuscript and offered suggestions that were wise and words of resonance that were encouraging.

The British writer Tim Dalgleish, who is working on a two-volume work on the poet Max Ehrmann, was uncommonly helpful in sharing his knowledge, research, and perspective on that mid-twentieth-century figure.

The late Phyllis Tickle, a dear friend to so many published and aspiring writers, was the first person who told me that this book was worth the investment of time and reflection. I will always be grateful for her friendship and encouragement.

A tapestry of friends including Kent Annan, Laura Bartlett, Michael Card, Sally Sampson Craft, Christopher de Vinck, Amanda Dykes, Jon Hirst, Sherrill Knezel, Mark McMinn, Ben Patterson, Scott Roley, Paul Santhouse, Heidi Maria Schmidt, David Smith, John Topliff, and Casey Tygrett have spoken into this manuscript in a variety of ways, directly and indirectly, in ways known and perhaps unknown. Thank you. To Cindy, Cynthia, Julia, and Sheri, I'm grateful to work alongside you in the world of words.

When I considered publishers with whom I might work on this project, one professional stood out among all of the others. I hoped I would have a chance to work with Lil Copan, an editor known for helping people craft the best book they could possibly write. Thank you, Lil, for saying yes. And thank you to the Broadleaf Books team for your design, editorial, sales, marketing, and publicity work. From my many years of work on your side of the desk, I know everything that goes into positioning a book well in the marketplace. I am grateful to each of you for your part in connecting words to readers.

To my mother, Nancy Crosby, whose perseverance, resilience, and steadfast love is an inspiration and model for me, I offer my deep gratitude. Thank you for reading an early version of this book and offering your wise feedback.

My family is my greatest treasure on earth. Thank you, Dustin and Jennifer, for being a son and daughter who I am proud of and learn from more with each passing year. Gillian and Nino, I am so grateful you became a part of our family those many years ago. And Ellie, Jack, Anna, Peggy, Tony, and Emily: I pray you will always be aware of the ways in which God meets *you* in the longings of your hearts.

Cindy Crosby, to whom this book is dedicated, models for me what an attentive life looks like, what the words of an artful writer read like, and what a life lived fully and with integrity means. Thank you for your encouragement throughout the writing process, and for understanding many late nights spent at the writing desk upstairs. *I love you to the moon and back.*

Ordinary Time, 2022

NOTES

Epigraph

Whenever we listen to the loamy contralto: Jennifer Maier, "Saudade," in *Now, Now* (Pittsburgh: University of Pittsburgh Press, 2013), 48–49.

Introduction

The music of your life is subtle and elusive: Frederick Buechner, *Sacred Journey* (San Francisco: HarperSanFrancisco, 1982), 77.

A melancholic longing or nostalgia: David Robson, "The Untranslatable Emotions You Never Knew You Had," *BBC Future*, January 26, 2017.

I remember a curious word that appeared: Heidi Maria Schmidt, interview with author, August 2020.

What we do with our longings: Ronald Rolheiser, *The Holy Longing* (New York: Doubleday, 1999), 5.

Whenever you find tears in your eyes: Frederick Buechner, *Whistling in the Dark* (San Francisco: HarperSanFrancisco, 1988), 105.

Part I

Ultimately, our yearning for God: Gerald G. May, *Addiction and Grace* (San Francisco: HarperSanFrancisco, 1988), 92.

Chapter 1

I was meant to walk these rails: Lyrics from "The Railwalker" by Brooks Williams used by permission of the composer. All rights reserved.

We are a people in the business of trying: Christopher de Vinck, *Moments of Grace* (Mahwah, NJ: Paulist Press, 2011), 150.

A feeling of home [that] permeates my memories: John S. Allen, *Home: How Habitat Made Us Human* (New York: Basic Books, 2015), 246.

It doesn't matter how fervently the spiritualized among us: Craig Barnes, *Searching for Home* (Grand Rapids: Brazos, 2003), 14.

The drawback was the beauty of Oregon: Mark McMinn, interview with author, August 2020.

It doesn't matter where you move: Barnes, *Searching for Home*, 14.

Chapter 2

Only when the pain of our dividedness becomes more than we can bear: Parker Palmer, *A Hidden Wholeness* (San Francisco: Jossey-Bass, 2004), 39.

We arrive in this world undivided: Palmer, *Hidden Wholeness*, 39.

I pay a steep price: Palmer, *Hidden Wholeness*, 39.

The mechanics of the Möbius strip are mysterious: Palmer, *Hidden Wholeness*, 47.

My friends, I believe that Christianity happens: Brennan Manning, *Lion and Lamb* (Grand Rapids, MI: Revell Books, 1986).

I believe Jesus calls all of us: Manning, *Lion and Lamb*, 64.

For the inconsistent, unsteady disciples: Brennan Manning, *The Ragamuffin Gospel* (Sisters, OR: Multnomah, 1990), 12.

In the midst of this world the Son of God: Henri J. M. Nouwen, *Making All Things New* (San Francisco: HarperOne, 1981), 93–94.

In the presence of God when we can listen to his voice: Nouwen, *Making All Things New,* 93–94.

Grace and gratitude belong together: Karl Barth, *Church Dogmatics,* 4/1, *The Doctrine of Reconciliation* (Edinburgh: T&T Clark, 1980), 41.

Chapter 3

But all the while, there was one thing we most needed: Robert Farrar Capon, *Between Noon and Three* (Grand Rapids: Eerdmans, 1982), 149.

The 1989 convention showcased new books for that fall season: Edwin McDowell, "Booksellers Convention Gains in Foreign Flavor," *New York Times,* June 3, 1989, 37.

A diffuse, unpleasant, vague sense of apprehension: B. J. Sadock, V. A. Sadock, and P. Ruiz, *Kaplan and Sadock's Synopsis of Psychiatry,* 11th ed. (Philadelphia: Wolters Kluwer, 2015), quoted in Sheryl Ankrom, "The Difference between Fear and Anxiety," Verywell Mind, July 8, 2020, https://tinyurl.com/bdz3u4yz.

She cites a statistic: Margaret Wehrenberg, *10 Best-Ever Anxiety Management Tips* (New York: W. W. Norton, 2009), xiii.

God is present with me in the midst of my anxieties: Howard Thurman, *Meditations of the Heart* (1953; repr., Boston: Beacon Press, 1981), 50.

We are called—we are urged: Henri J. M. Nouwen, *Following Jesus* (New York: Convergent Books, 2019), 83.

Similarly, in this life we are always waiting: Carmen Acevedo Butcher, "Walking the Stations of the Cross," The Center for Christian Ethics at Baylor University, 2013, 58.

Be not afraid: Robert J. Dufford, SJ, from the St. Louis Jesuits recording *Earthen Vessels,* 1975, administered by Oregon Catholic Press, permission pending.

Next to the Word of God: Martin Luther, *Luther's Works,* vol. 53, *Liturgy and Hymns* (St. Louis: Concordia Publishing, 1968), 323.

As Adele Calhoun noted: Adele Ahlberg Calhoun, *Spiritual Disciplines Handbook* (Downers Grove, IL: InterVarsity Press, 2005), 59.

A person dwells in a state of consolation: Vinita Hampton Wright, "Consolation and Desolation," Ignatian Spirituality, https://tinyurl.com/cc5peaka, retrieved March 5, 2021.

By contrast, Wright says: Wright, "Consolation and Desolation."

I love [the examen's] focus on gratitude: Marilyn McEntyre, *Where the Soul Alights* (Grand Rapids: Eerdmans, 2021), 53.

The questions of the examen open our attention: Calhoun, *Spiritual Disciplines Handbook*, 53.

Some of us have repressed this desire: Gerald G. May, *Addiction and Grace* (San Francisco: HarperSanFrancisco, 1988), 1.

Chapter 4

Forgiving is love's revolution: Lewis B. Smedes, *Forgive and Forget* (New York: Harper & Row, 1984), 94.

Connected people from all walks of life: G. C. Murphy Co., "History," gcmurphy.org/history.html, retrieved on September 5, 2020.

Weathered two world wars: Jason Togyer, *For the Love of Murphy's: The Behind-the-Counter Story of a Great American Retailer* (University Park: Pennsylvania State University Press, 2008), 249.

The late folk musician: Nanci Griffith, "Love at the Five and Dime," *The MCA Years, A Retrospective*, MCA Records, 1993.

By grace you have been saved: Renovaré Life with God Bible, NRSV, New Testament (New York: HarperBibles, 2005), 339.

I took my backpack: Adam Hamilton, *Forgiveness: Finding Peace through Letting Go* (Nashville: Abingdon Press, 2012), 15.

Create an ever-widening gap: Hamilton, *Forgiveness*, 15.

Forgiving someone means taking this thing you held on to: Jeanne Bishop, *Grace in the Rubble* (Grand Rapids: Zondervan, 2020), 170.

In the Truth and Reconciliation Commission: Desmond Tutu and Mpho Tutu, *The Book of Forgiving* (San Francisco: HarperOne, 2014), 5.

Usually takes a cast of two: Lewis B. Smedes, *The Art of Forgiving* (New York: Moorings, 1996), 95.

We feel a need to forgive ourselves: Smedes, *Art of Forgiving*, 95.

We all want to live in peace and harmony: Tutu and Tutu, *Book of Forgiving*, 209.

Chapter 5

The longing of every heart: Steve Garber, *The Seamless Life* (Downers Grove, IL: InterVarsity Press, 2020), 121.

The seed of the jack pine will not be given up: Howard Thurman, *Meditations of the Heart* (1953; repr., Boston: Beacon Press, 1981), 82–83.

Deep within the human spirit: Thurman, *Meditations of the Heart*, 82–83.

Lord, let my heart be good soil: Lyrics to the hymn "Good Soil" by Handt Hanson, copyright 1985, Prince of Peace Publishing, Changing Church, Inc. Used with the permission of Changing Church, Inc. All rights reserved.

Lord, let my heart be good soil: Hanson, "Good Soil."

A little more aware of the deeper, unnamed feelings: T. S. Eliot, *The Use of Poetry and the Use of Criticism* (London: Faber & Faber, 1933), 155.

When we despair of gaining inner transformation: Richard J. Foster, *Celebration of Discipline* (San Francisco: HarperSanFrancisco, 1978), 5.

Inner righteousness is a gift from God: Foster, *Celebration of Discipline*, 5.

She teaches that while we can (and should) be open: Ruth Haley Barton, *Sacred Rhythms* (Downers Grove, IL: InterVarsity Press), 11.

The journey of transformation begins: Stephen Smith, *Transformation of a Man's Heart* (Downers Grove, IL: InterVarsity Press, 2006), 15–16.

Transformation is less disorienting: Katie Haseltine, *All the Things: A 30-Day Guide to Experiencing God's Presence in the Prayer of Examen* (New York: Morgan James Faith Publishing, 2021), 206.

Down through Christian history: Bob Benson and Michael W. Benson, *Disciplines of the Inner Life* (Waco, TX: Word Books, 1985), ix.

Chapter 6

Long ago, a wise spiritual director said: Ruth Haley Barton, "Make a Joyful Silence," Transforming Center, https://transformingcenter.org/2009/02/make-a-joyful-silence/, retrieved December 11, 2021.

On the surface of it: Travis Scholl, *Walking a Labyrinth* (Downers Grove, IL: InterVarsity Press, 2014), 34.

Used as a preliminary petition: "Kyrie," *Encyclopaedia Britannica,* at Britanica.com, published April 28, 2017, retrieved November 14, 2021.

Kyrie, Setting 8: *Evangelical Lutheran Worship* (Minneapolis: Augsburg Fortress, 2006).

Then, in April of 1970: "History," Belmont Prairie, https://tinyurl.com/369bpd5k, retrieved December 2020.

The Psalms embrace the wide experience: *Renovaré Life with God Bible,* NRSV, Old Testament (New York: HarperBibles, 2005), 773–74.

In the last analysis: Thomas Merton, quoted in Ian Stackhouse, *Praying Psalms* (Eugene, OR: Cascade Books, 2018), vii.

Changed lives must implement the mission of peace: Mark O. Hatfield, *Conflict and Conscience* (Waco, TX: Word Books, 1971), 49–50.

Most cherished hours for writing: Bertha K. Ehrmann, *Max Ehrmann: A Poet's Life* (Boston: Bruce Humphries, 1951), 72.

Go placidly amid the noise: Max Ehrmann, "Desiderata," from *Desiderata: Words for Life* (public domain).

Part II

We long for a world of goodness: Curtis Thompson, *The Soul of Desire* (Downers Grove, IL: InterVarsity Press, 2021), 13.

Chapter 7

The more thankfully we daily receive: Dietrich Bonhoeffer, *Life Together* (New York: Harper & Row, 1954), 30.

Community cannot take root in a divided life: Parker Palmer, *The Courage to Teach* (San Francisco: Jossey-Bass Publishers, 1998), 92.

And the call is to community: Lyric from Michael Card song, "The Basin and the Towel," used with the permission of Mole End Music. All rights reserved.

Community is an ongoing entering into friendship: Bishop Seraphim Sigrist, *A Life Together: Wisdom of Community from the Christian East* (Brewster, MA: Paraclete Press, 2011), 13–14.

We best express God's nature: Adele Ahlberg Calhoun, *Spiritual Disciplines Handbook* (Downers Grove, IL: InterVarsity Press, 2005), 131.

Chapter 8

There's a marked difference: Maya Angelou, quoted in Marcia Ann Gillespie, "Sister Circle: Maya Angelou on the Power of Friendships," *Essence Magazine*, October 27, 2020.

In everyone's life: John O'Donohue, *Anam Cara: A Book of Celtic Wisdom* (New York: Cliff Street Books/HarperCollins, 1997), 14.

At the core of what makes an anamchara: Gary Crites, "The Head of the Body of Christ: Soul Friendship and Celtic Missionary Impulse," *Christian History* 132 (2019): 15.

Soul friends are not content: Keith Anderson, *Friendships That Run Deep* (Downers Grove, IL: InterVarsity Press, 1997), 122.

Ordinary friendships: Mindy Caliguire, *Spiritual Friendship* (Downers Grove, IL: InterVarsity Press, 2007), 17.

A friend is one who knows you: David Smith, *Men without Friends* (Nashville: Thomas Nelson, 1990), 212.

Henri's death has confirmed for me: Christopher de Vinck, *Nouwen Then* (Grand Rapids: Zondervan, 1999), 77.

Fred dearly loved his wife: Christopher de Vinck, personal conversation.

There are some people in our lives whose name we know: Dane Ortlund, *Gentle and Lowly* (Wheaton, IL: Crossway, 2020), 115.

Chapter 9

How do we come to choose: Robert Benson, *Between the Dreaming and the Coming True* (San Francisco: HarperSanFrancisco, 1996), 88.

How we spend our days: Annie Dillard, *The Writing Life* (New York: Harper & Row, 1989), xx.

In the primary biography of Chalmers: Nigel M. de S. Cameron, *Dictionary of Scottish Church History and Theology* (Downers Grove, IL: IVP, 1993), 160.

The grand essentials of happiness: Ben Patterson, *The Grand Essentials* (Waco, TX: Word, 1987), 13.

We have to recover a sense: Patterson, *Grand Essentials*, 85.

The hope of the resurrection: Patterson, *Grand Essentials*, 144.

The former is the longer, deeper story: Steven Garber, *The Seamless Life* (Downers Grove, IL: InterVarsity Press, 2020), 43.

There is no such thing as the instant leader: Bill George and Peter Sims, *True North* (San Francisco: Jossey-Bass, 2007), xx.

How do we come to choose: Benson, *Between the Dreaming and the Coming True*, 88.

We spend our days doing what we do: Benson, *Between the Dreaming and the Coming True*, 88.

Vocation at its deepest level: Parker J. Palmer, *Let Your Life Speak* (San Francisco: Jossey-Bass, 2000), 25.

Part III

The Christian vision of heaven affirms: Alister McGrath, *A Brief History of Heaven* (Oxford: Blackwell, 2003), 183.

Chapter 10

I believe heaven is the home: Christopher de Vinck, *Finding Heaven: Stories of Going Home* (Chicago: Loyola Press Chicago, 2002), 19.

While suicides often take place in isolation: Albert Y. Hsu, *Grieving a Suicide* (Downers Grove, IL: InterVarsity, 2017), 9.

If I find myself a desire: C. S. Lewis, *Mere Christianity* (San Francisco: HarperOne, 1980), 136–37.

Yes, heaven means hope: Lee Strobel, *The Case for Heaven* (Grand Rapids: Zondervan, 2021), 224.

The imagery used to portray heaven: Leland Ryken, James C. Wilhoit, and Tremper Longman III, *The Dictionary of Biblical Imagery* (Downers Grove, IL: IVP Academic, 1998), 372.

The single most important fact: Scot McKnight, *The Heaven Promise* (Colorado Springs, CO: Waterbrook, 2015), 15.

McKnight goes on to give his personal statement of belief: McKnight, *Heaven Promise*, 187–95.

Believe heaven is the home: de Vinck, *Finding Heaven*, 19.

The longing for heaven: Alister McGrath, *A Brief History of Heaven* (Oxford: Blackwell, 2003), 115.

It came to me spontaneously: Yo-Yo Ma interview with Jeffrey Brown, *PBS News Hour*, March 18, 2020.

In heaven what we want: Mark R. McMinn, *Finding Our Way Home* (San Francisco: Jossey-Bass, 2005), 172.

Far from the mad crowd: Lyrics to "We Will Dance Someday" written by Brooks Williams and published by Red Guitar Blue Music. Used with permission of the composer. All rights reserved.

Epilogue

We are people of desire: Curtis Thompson, *The Soul of Desire* (Downers Grove, IL: InterVarsity Press, 2021), 10.

Ever since I was a child: Jeffrey Tacklind, *The Winding Path of Transformation* (Downers Grove, IL: InterVarsity Press, 2019), 7.

For Longing: "For Longing," in *Benedictus: A Book of Blessings* (London: Bantam Press, 2007), 53.

RECOMMENDED READING FOR FURTHER STUDY AND REFLECTION

I believe that books are a primary source for reflecting on and getting in touch with the longings of our hearts and the ways in which we are met there by One who is full of grace. The following list represents just three books for each of the ten longings found in *The Language of the Soul*, though many others could be chosen. Look for more reading cited in the endnotes section, as well. It is my hope that the reading of this book will prompt you to go deeper through others such as those noted here.

Overview of Longing and Desire:

- Curtis Thompson, *The Soul of Desire* (IVP, 2021)
- Ronald Rolheiser, *The Holy Longing: The Search for a Christian Spirituality* (Doubleday, 1999)
- Jen Pollock Michel, *Teach Us to Want: Longing, Ambition, and the Life of Faith* (IVP Crescendo, 2014)

Home:

- Frederick Buechner, *The Longing for Home* (HarperSanFrancisco, 1996)
- Craig M. Barnes, *Searching for Home: Spirituality for Restless Souls* (Brazos Press, 2003)

- Mark R. McMinn, *Finding Our Way Home: Turning Back to What Matters Most* (Jossey-Bass, 2005)

An Undivided Life:

- Parker Palmer, *A Hidden Wholeness: The Journey toward an Undivided Life* (Jossey-Bass, 2004)
- Chuck DeGroat, *Wholeheartedness: Busyness, Exhaustion, and Healing the Divided Self* (Eerdmans, 2016)
- David Benner, *The Gift of Being Yourself* (InterVarsity Press, 2004)

Freedom from Fear and Anxiety:

- Henri J. M. Nouwen, *Following Jesus: Finding Our Way Home in an Age of Anxiety* (Convergent, 2019)
- Gareth Higgins, *How Not to Be Afraid: Seven Ways to Live When Everything Seems Terrifying* (Broadleaf Books, 2021)
- Dr. Margaret Wehrenberg, *The Ten Best Anxiety Busters: Simple Strategies to Take Control of Your Worry* (W. W. Norton, 2015)

Forgiveness:

- Desmond Tutu and Mpho Tutu, *The Book of Forgiving: The Four-Fold Path for Healing Ourselves and Our World* (HarperOne, 2014)
- Lewis B. Smedes, *Forgive and Forget* (Harper & Row, 1984)

- Marcia Ford, *The Sacred Art of Forgiveness: Forgiving Ourselves and Others through God's Grace* (Skylight Paths Publishing, 2006)

Spiritual Transformation:

- Ruth Haley Barton, *Invitation to Solitude and Silence: Experiencing God's Transforming Presence* (Formatio, 2010)
- Henri J. M. Nouwen, *The Return of the Prodigal Son* (Doubleday, 1992)
- James Bryan Smith, *The Good and Beautiful God* (Formatio, 2009)

Peace:

- Henri Nouwen, *Finding My Way Home: Pathways to Life and the Spirit* (Crossroad, 2001)
- Abide Christian Meditation, *Peace with the Psalms: 40 Readings to Relax Your Mind and Calm Your Heart* (Zondervan, 2021)
- Christian Wiman, *My Bright Abyss: Meditations of a Modern Believer* (Farrar, Straus and Giroux, 2013)

Community:

- Bishop Seraphim Sigrist, *A Life Together: Wisdom of Community from the Christian East* (Paraclete Press, 2011)

- Jamie Arpin-Ricci, *The Cost of Community: Jesus, St. Francis and Life in the Kingdom* (InterVarsity Press, 2011)
- Dietrich Bonhoeffer, *Life Together* (Harper & Row, 1954)

Friendship:

- John O'Donohue, *Anam Cara: A Book of Celtic Wisdom* (Cliff Street Books/HarperCollins, 1997)
- Mindy Caliguire, *Spiritual Friendship* (Formatio, 2007)
- Suzanne Stabile, *The Path Between Us* (Formatio, 2018)

Meaningful Work:

- Gregory S. Clapper, *Living Your Heart's Desire: God's Call and Your Vocation* (Upper Room Books, 2005)
- Ben Patterson, *The Grand Essentials* (Word Publishing, 1987)
- Parker Palmer, *Let Your Life Speak: Listening to the Voice of Vocation* (Jossey-Bass, 2000)

Heaven:

- Elyse Fitzpatrick, *Home: How Heaven and the New Earth Satisfy Our Deepest Longings* (Bethany House, 2016).

- Scot McKnight, *The Heaven Promise: Engaging the Bible's Truth about the Life to Come* (Waterbrook, 2015).
- N. T. Wright, *Surprised by Hope* (HarperOne, 2008)